Overcoming Africa's 10 Plagues

PRAYER COMPANION FOR

'Africa's Industrialisation & Prosperity
From Esau Syndrome to Structural Adjustment Strategy'

Overcoming
Africa's
10 Plagues

Bloodshed, Witch craft, Tribalism, Sanitation,
Poverty, Disease, Famine, Corruption, Ignorance,
Loss of Generations & Mineral Wealth

DAVID SSEPPUUYA

ISBN 978-9970-556-00-7

Produced and published by:
Beeranga Mwesigwa Foundation
Suite B1, Adam House, Plot 11, Portal Avenue,
Kampala, Uganda
E-mail: mwesigwafoundation@gmail.com

Dedication

This book is dedicated to
all intercessors who continue
to pray for Africa.

Acknowledgements

This book is the outline of a prophetic message that seeks to lay the spiritual foundation for the redemption of Africa's economies. It is an intercessory companion for a bigger book, 'Africa's Industrialisation & Prosperity – From Esau Syndrome to Structural Adjustment Strategy', a publication inspired by the Holy Spirit to address Africa's incessant economic challenges. The truths are the Holy Spirit's, He Who guides us into all truth (John 16:13), while the opinions, alongside any errors, are mine and I would take full responsibility. Quotations and citations are accurate in as far as they are rendered.

I am grateful to my wife Julia, and the children, for their support and patience in seeing through these two projects. I am also indebted to Apostle Victor Uchegbulam, Dr Steve Ogan, Pastor Laban Jjumba, and Dr James Magara for their work in showing us the spiritual horizons of Africa, and to Rev. Canon Christine Shimanya for the shepherding and prayer support. I thank the Lord for Dr Joe Ibojie of Aberdeen, Scotland, for his teaching on meanings of prophetic symbols. I am thankful to Mr Charles Kintu for his dedication and skill in addressing the technical issues of our publishing projects. I am grateful to Pastor Jjumba for graciously accepting to write the foreword, for which he has the spiritual insights.

Most of all I acknowledge the Hand of our Lord Jesus Christ, whose message this is.

Contents

Foreword

David Sseppuuya has seen a very revealing parallel between God's judgments upon ancient Egypt and the disasters, pandemics, curses and catastrophes that the Continent of Africa and black people everywhere are plagued with today.

As I read through the manuscript I could not help seeing God's hand of judgment upon us Africans due to our deep commitment to idolatry. I could also feel the burden on God's heart as He wonders whether we will see the connection between our idolatrous behaviour and His heavy hand of judgment, so that we can turn to Him in repentance to receive healing.

God's judgments are redemptive. God is not a sadist. He does not enjoy seeing people writhing in pain. Like a parent punishing a child as a corrective measure to instil discipline and morals, God goes through the pain of dispensing His judgments upon communities with the hope that they will learn righteousness. "... For when Your judgments are in the earth, the inhabitants of the world will learn righteousness." (Isaiah 26:9b)

I am hoping that by seeing the connection between God's judgments upon Egypt and our experiences as Africans and the black race, we will indeed see that it is God, beckoning us to turn from our idolatrous ways, repent and turn to Him for healing. When we do not see God's finger in our sufferings, we will continue to blame it on colonialism, discrimination, injustice, etcetera. Indeed there is discrimination and injustice. Nevertheless, our suffering is more than these external manifestations.

When God manifested His signs and began His judgments in ancient Egypt, with Moses' rod turning into a snake, the Nile water turning into blood and then frogs turning up and filling the land; when Pharaoh's magicians mimicked those signs and miracles, Pharaoh's heart was hardened. He concluded those acts could have had other explanations apart from being the finger of God's judgment upon Egypt.

However, when the plague of lice was unleashed upon the land, and Pharaoh's magicians could not mimick it, the magicians confirmed to Pharaoh that this was "the finger of God."

This book is the voice of a herald announcing that the pains and troubles that Africa and the Africans are undergoing are the finger of God's judgment. The book traces many centuries of Africa's history and lists plague after plague, war after war, and catastrophe after catastrophe, quoting all the documented statistics. The book shows the symbolic and prophetic resemblance of these to the plagues of ancient Egypt. The book then provides a detailed way to bring repentance before God and to pray for Africa's healing and restoration.

I wholeheartedly recommend this book as a prayer manual to address the issues that have plagued Africa for so long.

Laban Jjumba,
Senior Pastor Emeritus, *Deliverance Church Kansanga*, Kampala, and East African Regional Coordinator, *Intercessors for Africa*.

Introduction

It was the 14th of February 2015, and I was seated in the hotel room studying the scriptures when revelation started streaming interminably. I had arrived in the Tanzanian port city of Dar es Salaam three days earlier, setting myself to continue, from a distance, the season of prayer my fellowship back in Kampala, Uganda had begun a fortnight before.

Now on my own in Tanzania, I was continuing with the study of the Old Testament through the year, and I was in the early chapters of the book of Exodus. Suddenly, out of the scriptures jumped meaning of incredible depth. Revelation and fresh meaning was springing forth from the ancient scripture account of the exodus of the Hebrews from Egypt. In my spiritual walk I had been exposed to teaching that showed that occasionally biblical reference to Egypt does point to Africa, and so I had had to learn to ask the Lord for discernment as to which meaning – the continent or the country - a particular reference was being made.

I had come to Tanzania to spend 4-6 months with the World Bank and so, in a sense, my mind was tuned to matters of development economics. Besides my professional work as a journalist which compelled me to be a critical observer of society, I was also, at a spiritual level, part of a growing number of Africans that were concerned about the continent's direction, or lack of it. With Africa fairing particularly badly on all human development fronts and, conviction having come to the

Body of Christ that we seek the Lord, a lot of prayer was being invested in intercession for divine intervention in our economic plight. Those who are spiritually alert had discerned God as saying that He was going to redeem the continent. The Lord's word for Africa is, after all, a promise contained in the Bible. How and when that redemption would come has remained central to prayer and petition.

For a few years before this I had picked up intellectual and spiritual insights into the welfare of Africa which I would pen in a regular newspaper column. By and by, the papers stopped running the column, but the insights continued, and I would simply file them away, backed by research to corroborate and authenticate them. In July 2014, while on a prayer journey to Israel, I shared with Dr Steve Ogan, one of the leaders of Intercessors for Africa/ Africa House of Prayer, snippets of what I had received. "Write a book", was his commanded advice.

As I backed up what I had received with research, and set myself to write the book on African economies, I realised that the reason the Lord had opened doors for me with the World Bank (I had spent part of 2012 and most of 2013 consulting with the World Bank in Kampala, Uganda, before the same institution invited me to spend half of 2015 with its office in Tanzania) was to equip me with a better understanding of the economies of Africa.

Thus when I arrived in Dar es Salaam on 11 February 2015, I knew that alongside the World Bank consultancy, I was on divine assignment to seek to understand development economics better so as to write the book on how Africa can get out of poverty. The tentative title was 'How Africa

Will Industrialise and Prosper'. It is at this point that the Holy Spirit begun to add the spiritual dimension, from the book of Exodus, to the immense insights He had already started to reveal on the technical aspects of our economies.

Through the rest of February and into early March, the Lord showed how the plagues of Exodus chapters 7 to 11 were an exact fit of the state of Africa today. Trembling with the fear of the Almighty and with excitement about the incredible depth of what I would name the 'Plagues Revelation', I determined to share it with the Intercessors for Africa. That year, the Africa House of Prayer conference was scheduled to be held in Mombasa, Kenya, just up the Indian Ocean coast from where I was, and so I drew up a plan to make the short hop. But the Lord said, "No! Not yet," and so I cancelled my plans.

I eventually got to understand why. The Plagues Revelation was being unveiled over a long stretch of time (in the end it took two years, with the latest revelation – the corresponding judgments of Isaiah 19:1-18 – falling in place in February 2017). In my hotel room on the morning of Sunday 22 February 2015, during the first prayer watch of the day, the instruction came that I should write the revelation in a book to be entitled, *"The Plagues of Africa – a Prayer Companion for 'Deindustrialising Africa: How Esau Syndrome with Minerals Undermines Nations' Transformation. Why Industrial Revolution Must Happen'."* The title has since been modified and edited with the guidance of the Holy Spirit.

Following is a summary of the Plagues Revelation and the Post-Exodus Judgments as they link directly in the overall prophetic picture about Africa. It is designed to be used as an intercessory manual. To better appreciate the context in which it has been revealed, and in order to pray with understanding, it is advisable to read alongside it the main book, *'Africa's Industrialisation & Prosperity – From Esau Syndrome to Structural Adjustment Strategy'*, for which the Lord has provided the grace to write and publish simultaneously.

David Sseppuuya
Kampala, Uganda,
March 2017
dsseppuuya@yahoo.com

CHAPTER ONE

'Egypt' as Africa

Egypt is mentioned more than 750 times in scripture; 'Pharaoh', the title of Egypt's king, occurs more than 200 times in the Bible. The mention of Egypt is sometimes in the positive and sometimes in the negative. The mention of Egypt varies – at times it refers to the geographical bounds that are roughly modern-day Egypt in northeast Africa/southern Middle East or, indeed, to a much wider geopolitical spread.

Egypt was the southern neighbour of Israel/Canaan, and was one of the seven powers of the ancient world, alongside Assyria, Babylon, Medo-Persia, Greece, Rome and the Hittite Empire.

The most famous of the Egypt-Israel relationships is the bondage, from which the Exodus was birthed. What is frequently forgotten is that the arrival of Israel into Egypt came with the invitation of Egypt, through its Prime Minister Joseph and the approval of Pharaoh. There were times when Israel turned to Egypt when looking for a safe haven during crisis times, or for food during a famine. Abraham/Abram (Genesis 12:10-20) fled to Egypt to escape the famine, while Jacob sent his sons across to look for food (Genesis 42). Joseph took his young family, including the Baby Jesus, to Egypt to escape Herod's murderous intentions (Matthew 2:13-23).

What, then, is this geographical entity Egypt? Like all the ancient empires, Egypt's borders expanded and contracted with the ebb and flow of geopolitical power. Conquests would carry the boundaries farther out; assimilation of conquered peoples would multiply the population many-fold. Counter-conquests would shrink kingdoms again.

Egypt today is a transcontinental country spanning the northeast corner of Africa and southwest corner of Asia. In ancient days, the borders were equally fluid, depending on the reach of the power of the Pharaoh on the throne.

For instance the 500 years between 1500 BC and 1000 BC was one of the most successful chapters in Ancient Egypt's history, when the empire stretched into Palestine and Syria in the north and Nubia in the south.[i] It is during this period, in 1446 BC, that the Exodus of the Israelites happened. It had also been during this time that the great temple complexes at Luxor and in the Valley of the Kings were constructed. The Bible gives account of what was happening at this time: "So they put slave masters over them to oppress them with forced labour, and they built Pithom and Rameses as store cities for Pharaoh" (Exodus 1:11). The name Rameses refers to the great Egyptian Pharaoh Rameses II[ii]. Pharaoh Rameses II is also one of the more popular candidates for Pharaoh of the Exodus, though the period of his reign, 1279-1213 BC, rules him out of the event which took place in 1446 BC.

Before that, in the period 2500 BC to 1500 BC, Egyptian civilisation had experienced periods of strength and unity, and also of weakness and division.[iii] Yet the period after, from 1000 BC to 500 BC Egypt had been invaded and occupied by several different peoples including the Persians in 525 BC. It had become merely one amongst many provinces of the huge Persian empire, which is mentioned in Esther 1:1.

Therefore at the time of Israelite bondage and the exodus, Egypt was at its most powerful, measured by the size of its territory. It is territory that stretched deep and wide to envelope regions that are part of other nations of modern-day Africa.

The more acceptable Pharaoh of the Exodus, Thutmose III, who has also been called the 'Napoleon of Ancient Egypt'[iv], is recorded to have "expanded the boundaries of Egyptian influence far beyond natural borders"[v].

Therefore if the great, conquering Pharaoh Thutmose III was the potentate to whom the appeal, "Go to Pharaoh and speak to him, 'Thus says the LORD, the God of the Hebrews, "Let My people go, that they may serve Me" (Exodus 7:2), and repeated in 7:16; 8:1; 9:1; 9:13; and 10:3, then this appeal would have been going out to dozens if not scores of leaders who were representing Pharaoh in the districts and provinces of the powerful empire.

The government structure was arranged as a pyramid, so to speak, with the Pharaoh at the top of the apex, alongside the gods, who Egyptians believed to be in control of the universe. Pharaohs were believed to be gods in human form. Pharaoh appointed a chief minister called a vizier as a supervisor – Joseph held that position (Genesis 41:41 – 50:26). Working with the vizier were scribes, high-level employees, who kept government records. Below the pharaoh nobles and priests - only nobles could hold government posts; priests were responsible for pleasing the gods.

In Egypt's vassal states further south, like Nubia (in present-day Sudan/South Sudan) and the Kushite Empire (which covers some of Sudan and parts of present-day Ethiopia) the Pharaoh's authority would have been exercised locally by chiefs, which would ring many parts of modern-day Africa into the Egypt to which the appeal to free God's people was made.

What is Egypt? There is the modern state, well-demarcated on contemporary maps, but there is also the ancient empire that is mentioned in the Bible. In the original Hebrew text, the name of the country/kingdom/empire is Mitsrayim or Mizraim[vi]. The term Egypt was once used to mean the entire Africa[vii], which in scripture is referred to as the Land of Ham: "Then Israel entered Egypt; Jacob lived as an alien in the land of Ham" (Psalms 105:23). A contemporary near-parallel is the name America: When one mentions America today, the basic understanding is that that's reference to the United States (of Donald Trump, Mickey Mouse and McDonald's). Yet Canada is in America (North America), as is Mexico. To the south of North America is another continent, South/Latin America that also identifies with the same proper noun. So our comprehension of what Egypt is should not be limited by certain geographical bounds or modern maps, but ought to be open-minded enough to discern what the specific reference is alluding to.

The other original names for Africa include the Land of Cush or Ethiopia and the Land of Havilah. Ethiopia is the Greek equivalent of the Hebrew name Cush[viii], and it took precedence when the Bible was translated into the Greek in 250 BC. In the Table of Nations in Genesis 10, which outlines, among others, the account of Noah's sons, Havilah is identified as a son to Cush: "The sons of Ham: Cush, Mizraim, Put and Canaan. The sons of Cush: Seba, Havilah, Sabtah, Raamah and Sabteca. The sons of Raamah: Sheba and Dedan. Cush was the father of Nimrod, who grew to be a mighty warrior on the earth. He was a mighty hunter before the LORD; that is why it is said, 'Like Nimrod, a mighty hunter before the LORD.'"

The land of Ham is in the region of Africa where Ham's sons, Cush and Mizraim, settled. "Some of their descendants seem to have moved to other regions, but generally Africa came to be known as the Land of Ham. The original Mizraim was a descendant of Ham. The present-day Arab Republic of Egypt, most of whom are Semitic, being cousins of Israel through Abraham's concubine Hagar, are not descendants of Ham. The first Arabs came into the area of Egypt much later. Because of the migrations of African peoples, the descendants of Cush and Mizraim have scattered all over the continent, and many have scattered around the world, either by choice or by being sold into slavery."[ix]

God's redemptive plans for Africa are well-spelt out in scripture, particularly Isaiah 19: 19-25, which talks of the "witness to the Lord Almighty in the land of Egypt" and its blessing on the earth in concert with Israel and Assyria (Arab world).

Preceding this encouraging word in the same passage, the Prophet Isaiah had been used of the Lord to convey God's judgment on Egypt/Africa as outlined in verses 1 – 17. It is these judgments that find reflection in the plagues that precede the Exodus, which still have resonance in contemporary Africa. It is these judgements that talk about "what the Lord Almighty has planned against Egypt" (Isaiah 19:12b). The overriding theme of the book of Exodus is deliverance; what Pharaoh and Egypt ended up with was the very opposite – bondage. When discerned by the power of the Holy Spirit, it is apparent that the plagues still afflict Africa today.

The judgments of Isaiah 19:1-17 are centred mainly on the economic well-being of Egypt/Africa. The ten plagues of Exodus chapters 7 to 11 culminate in economic hardship, as is reflected in the pestilence on livestock (economic well-being), which is the only plague mentioned twice, being central in the Plague on Livestock (9:1-7) and secondary in the Plague on the Firstborn (11:5b).

Between the blessings of the promises of the prophecy of Isaiah 19:19-25 and the proclamation against Egypt that are spelt out in Isaiah 19:1-17 lies the fact that Pharaoh did not repent in sincerity during or after the period of the nine months[x] that the ten plagues had come upon Egypt (there was the occasional half-hearted "sorry" and requests to be blessed – Exodus 8:28; 9:27; 12:32 - but the man was essentially hardened of heart right up to the point his army drowned in the Red Sea, 14:27-28, while in pursuit of the redeemed Israelites).

It is therefore apparent that the fulfilment of the promises of the prophecy of Isaiah 19:19-25 will be contingent upon the requisite repentance being brought before the Lord.

It is then that the judgments pronounced in Exodus chapters 7 to 11, then reinforced in Isaiah 19:1-17, will be lifted.

(Endnotes)

i www.timemaps.com

ii The NIV Study Bible, Study Notes on Genesis 47:11

iii www.timemaps.com

iv Study Notes, the MacArthur Study Bible (NKJV)

v Ibid.

vi Peter Asiimwe, *The African Dream: A Compelling Strategic Vision.* Beeranga Mwesigwa Foundation, Kampala, 2016

vii Tokumboh Adeyemo, *Is Africa Cursed? A Vision for the Radical Transformation of An Ailing Continent.* WordAlive Publishers, Nairobi, 1997, 2009

viii Peter Asiimwe, *The African Dream: A Compelling Strategic Vision.* Beeranga Mwesigwa Foundation, Kampala, 2016

ix Laban Jjumba, *Let Africa My People Go.* Mwesigwa Foundation, Kampala, 2013

x Gareth Crossley, *The Old Testament Explained and Applied.* Evangelical Press, Darlington, England, 2002

CHAPTER TWO

Plague of Blood (Bloodshed & War)

Pharaonic Confrontation:

Exodus 7:14-25 ""14 So the LORD said to Moses: "Pharaoh's heart *is* hard; he refuses to let the people go. 15 Go to Pharaoh in the morning, when he goes out to the water, and you shall stand by the river's bank to meet him; and the rod which was turned to a serpent you shall take in your hand. 16 And you shall say to him, 'The LORD God of the Hebrews has sent me to you, saying, "Let My people go, that they may serve Me in the wilderness"; but indeed, until now you would not hear! 17 Thus says the LORD: "By this you shall know that I *am* the LORD. Behold, I will strike the waters which *are* in the river with the rod that *is* in my hand, and they shall be turned to blood. 18 And the fish that *are* in the river shall die, the river shall stink, and the Egyptians will loathe to drink the water of the river.""""

19 Then the LORD spoke to Moses, "Say to Aaron, 'Take your rod and stretch out your hand over the waters of Egypt, over their streams, over their rivers, over their

ponds, and over all their pools of water, that they may become blood. And there shall be blood throughout all the land of Egypt, both in *buckets of* wood and *pitchers of* stone.'" [20] And Moses and Aaron did so, just as the LORD commanded. So he lifted up the rod and struck the waters that *were* in the river, in the sight of Pharaoh and in the sight of his servants. And all the waters that *were* in the river were turned to blood. [21] The fish that *were* in the river died, the river stank, and the Egyptians could not drink the water of the river. So there was blood throughout all the land of Egypt.

[22] Then the magicians of Egypt did so with their enchantments; and Pharaoh's heart grew hard, and he did not heed them, as the LORD had said. [23] And Pharaoh turned and went into his house. Neither was his heart moved by this. [24] So all the Egyptians dug all around the river for water to drink, because they could not drink the water of the river. [25] And seven days passed after the LORD had struck the river."

Post-Exodus Judgment:

Isaiah 19:2 "I will set Egyptians against Egyptians; Everyone will fight against his brother, And everyone against his neighbour, city against city, kingdom against kingdom."

Snapshot: (Genocide & Massacres)

South Sudan: Ethnic violence, 2011 and on-going;

Sudan: Darfur Genocide, 400,000 killed, 2003-onwards; Lord's Resistance Army insurgency

Rwanda: Genocide, 800,000 killed, 1994; Massacres, 1973; Massacres, 1959

Burundi: Genocide, 80,000-120,000 killed, 1972; Genocide, 300,000 killed, 1993; Massacre on the Titanic Express, 2000; Itaba Massacre, 2002; Gatumba Massacre, 2004

Algeria: Setif and Guelma Massacre, 1945

Namibia: Herero Genocide, 65,000 out of 80,000 Herero killed, 1904-07

Zimbabwe: Matabeleland Massacre, 20,000-30,000 killed, 1983-87

Uganda: Mengo Crisis, 1966; State-inspired extrajudicial killings, 300,000-500,000 murdered, 1971-86; Barlonyo Massacre, 2004

Congo, DR: Colonial Atrocities, 1885-1905

South Africa: Weenen Massacre, 1838; Sharpeville Massacre, 1960; Soweto Uprising, 1976

Kenya: Mau Mau counter-insurgency, 90,000 killed; Post-election violence 2007/8, over 1,000 killed; Garissa Massacre, 1980; Wagalla Massacre, 1984;

Nigeria: Boko Haram massacres and suicide attacks/ Sharia Conflict, 1999-on-going frequent massacres

Sao Tome & Principe: Batepa Massacre, 1953

Ethiopia: Tens of thousands executed in Marxist pogroms, 1974-87

Tanzania/Tanganyika: 250,000 lives lost in post-Maji Maji rebellion man-induced famine, 1905[i]

Snapshot: (War & Conflict)

Egypt, Arab Republic: Six Day War, 1967; Yom Kippur War, 1973; Libyan-Egyptian War, 1977; Egyptian Revolution and Aftermath 2011; Sinai Insurgency, 2011 on-going

Egypt, Republic: Suez Crisis, 1956

Egypt, Kingdom: Mediterranean and Middle East theatre of World War II, 1940-45; Arab-Israel War, 1948

Egypt, Sultanate: Middle Eastern theatre of World War I, 1914-18

Egypt, Khedivate of: Mahdist War, 1881-99; Anglo-Egyptian War, 1882

Egypt, Eyaletf: Ottoman-Portuguese conflicts, 1538-1557; French Revolutionary wars, 1792-1802; Napoleonic wars 1803-1815; Anglo-Turkish War, 1807-1809

Egypt, Mamluk Sultanate: Alexandrian Crusade, 1365

Egypt, Ayyubid Dynasty: Ayyubids conquests of North Africa and Nubia, 1171-1172; The Crusades, 1095-1272

Egypt, Rashudin Caliphate: Muslim conquest of Egypt, 639-642

Egypt, Sassanid Empire: Sassanid conquest of Egypt, 618-621

Egypt, Roman Province: Final War of the Roman Republic, 32 BC – 30 BC

Egypt, Ptolemaic Kingdom: Wars of Alexander the Great, 335 BC – 323 BC

Egypt, Achaemenid Periods: Wars against Persian conquest, 530 BC – 323 BC

Egypt, New Kingdom: attacks from Libyans, 1206 BC – 1150 BC

Sudan (Sudan & South Sudan): South Sudanese civil war, 2013 and on-going; Second Sudanese Civil War, 1983-2005; First Sudanese Civil War, 1955-1972; Mahdist War, 1881-99; Roman Prefect of Egypt invades Kingdom of Cush, 23 BC; Pharaoh Ramses II fights in Nubia 1279 BC – 1213 BC

Algeria: Maghreb insurgency, 2002-on-going; Civil War, 1991-2002; Western Sahara conflict, 1970-on-going; Algerian War, 1954-62; World War II North Africa campaign, 1940-43; French Conquest, 1830-47; Capture of Algiers, 1529; Muslim Conquest of Maghreb, 647-709; Vandalic War, 533-534; Jugurthine War 112 BC-106 BC; Punic Wars 264 BC-146 BC

Somalia: Al-Shabaab insurgency, 2008 on-going; Somali Civil War, 1991 on-going; Ethio-Somali War, 1977; Italian conquest of British Somaliland, 1940; East African Campaign in World War II, 1940-41; Ethiopian-Adal War, 1529-1543; Invasion of Ancient Egypt by Kingdom of Cush and Land of Punt, 1700 BC

Ethiopia: Ethio-Somali War, 1977; East African Campaign in World War II, 1940-41; Second Italo-Abyssinian War, 1935-36; First Italo-Ethiopian War, 1895-96; Ethiopian-Adal War, 1529-43

Mauritius: Battle of Grand Port, 1810

Madagascar: Battle of Madagascar (World War II), 1942;

Madagascar Revolt, 1947-48

Rwanda: Civil War, 1990-94

Uganda: Buganda-Bunyoro wars, 18th and 19th centuries; Invasion from Tanzania, 1972; Uganda-Tanzania War, 1978-79; Civil War, 1981-86; Holy Spirit Movement insurgency, 1986-87; Lord's Resistance Army insurgency, 1987-2005

Kenya: Mau Mau Uprising, 1952-60; Shifta War, 1963-67

Tanzania: Uganda-Tanzania War, 1978-79; 26,000 killed in Maji Maji rebellion, 1905

Benin: France conquers Dahomey, 1889-94; Yoruba-Ashanti War, 1768;

Cameroon: Fula jihads, 1835-36; Fulani War, 1804-08

Cote d'Ivoire: Second Ivorian Civil War, 2010-11; First Ivorian Civil War, 2002-07; Mandingo Wars, 1883-98

Ghana: Accra Riots, 1948; War of the Golden Stool, 1900; Anglo-Ashanti wars 1823-31; Anglo-Dutch wars, 1664-65; Dutch-Portuguese War, 1620-54

Liberia: Second Liberian Civil War, 1999-2003; First Liberian Civil War, 1989-96

Mali: Northern Mali conflict, 2012-on-going; Third and Second Tuareg Rebellions, 2012/2007-09; Agacher Strip War, 1985; First Tuareg Rebellion, 1962-65; Mandingo Wars, 1883-86; Songhai conquers Mema, 1460s; Almoravid conquest of Ghana Empire, 1075; Muslim conquest of the Maghreb, 647-709

Mauritania: Western Sahara conflict, 1970-on-going

Niger: Tuareg Rebellion, 2012; Second Azawad insurgency, 2007-09; Insurgency in the Maghreb, 2002-on-going; First Azawad insurgency, 1990-95; Kaocen Revolt, 1916-17; Songhai Civil War, 1516-17

Nigeria: Sharia Conflict/Boko Haram, 1999-on-going; Nigerian (Biafra) Civil War, 1967-70; Benin Expedition, 1897; Rafin Jaki Jihad, 1873; Fula jihads, 1835-36; Fulani War, 1804-08; Oyo-Benin War, 1578-1608

Sierra Leone: Civil War, 1991-2002; Ndongboyosoi War, 1982

Central African Republic: Civil War, 2012-on-going; Resistance Army insurgency, 1987-on-going

Republic of Congo: Civil War, 1997-99; Kongo Civil War, 1665-1709

Democratic Republic of Congo: Katanga insurgency, 1987; Second Congo War, 1998-2003; First Congo War, 1996-97; Shaba II Rebellion, 1978; Shaba I Rebellion, 1977; ADF insurgency, 2007-on-going; Simba Rebellion, 1964; Congo Crisis, 1960-66

South Africa: South Africa border war with various neighbours, 1966-1990; Maritz Rebellion, 1914-15; Second Boer War, 1899-1902; First Boer War, 1880-81; Xhosa Wars, 1779-1879; Anglo-Zulu War, 1879; Great Trek conflicts, 1830s-1840s; Ndwandwe-Zulu War, 1817-19

Zimbabwe: Chimurenga/Rhodesian Bush War, 1964-79; Second Matabele War, 1896-97; First Matabele War, 1893-94

Mozambique: War of Independence, 1964-74; Civil War, 1977-92; Internal conflict, 2013-14

Angola: War of Independence, 1961-74; Civil War, 1975-2004

Namibia: Caprivi Conflict, 1994-99; War of Independence, 1966-90; Maritz Rebellion, 1914-15[ii]

Fact:

Fish is a big delicacy in Uganda, a country endowed with part of the world's second-largest fresh water lake, and from where the Nile, earth's longest river, starts its winding journey. In mid-1994, Ugandans stopped eating the delicacy, particularly the giant Nile Perch, because the fish in Lake Victoria were gorging themselves on human flesh. The flesh was that of some of the hundreds of thousands of Rwandese murdered in the Genocide and dumped in River Kagera, which empties into Lake Victoria.

Before that, on 22 November 1992, Leon Mugesera, a senior ideologue in the Rwanda government, had made a speech in which he publicly urged the Hutu to destroy the Tutsi and return them to their (mythical) ancestral home in Ethiopia "via the short cut of the Nyabarongo River", which feeds into the rivers of the Nile watershed. Of course as the White Nile flows northwards through Sudan, it meets with the Blue Nile that originates in Ethiopia.

Prophetic Implication:

Of the 362 passages in which the Hebrew word 'dam' (blood) occurs in the Old Testament, 203 refer to death with violence. Only six passages connect life and blood, and just 17 refer to eating meat with blood. It is clear then that death is the association most likely to be made by the use of the term blood.[iii]

That the pharaonic plague of blood that was in the River Nile makes it even more poignant, given the blood-letting resulting from socio-political conflict that is still evident in the Africa's Nile Basin today. The River Nile is representative of a big chunk of Africa, there being nine riverine states, and many others that are aquatically-intertwined with some of the world's greatest bodies. Rivers prophetically represent the flow of the Holy Spirit, so a pollution of blood in one of its biggest riverine systems implies danger for the continent. Blood filling the "wooden buckets and stone jars" (Exodus 7:19) implies judgment on the idolatrous faith of the Egyptians since they believed in gods and images made out of wood, stone and clay.

The Nile is very possibly Gihon, the second of the headwaters flowing from Eden (Genesis 2:10). Gihon is recorded to be "flowing around the entire land of Cush [Ethiopia/Sudan]" (Genesis 2:13). Gihon in Hebrew is a common noun meaning 'spurter'[iv]: to spurt or spurting is most commonly used in reference to the sudden gush of blood, which then makes a direct correlation with the Nile and the bloodiness that has coursed through its African journey over millennia.

God's Principle:

"Hands that shed innocent blood" (Proverbs 6:16-19) is one of six things that the Lord hates, seven that are an abomination to him. The Lord also declares that "Whoever sheds the blood of man, by man shall his blood be shed, for God made man in his own image" (Genesis

9:6). Murderers are slated for eternal damnation and are cursed, for the Lord says, respectively, that "Keep far from a false charge, and do not kill the innocent and righteous, for I will not acquit the wicked" (Exodus 23:7) and "'Cursed be anyone who takes a bribe to shed innocent blood.' And all the people shall say, 'Amen.'" (Deuteronomy 27:25). Most of all, God commanded: "You shall not murder" (Exodus 20:13)

Prayer Points:

1. Repentance: God has observed: "What have you done? The voice of your brother's blood is crying to me from the ground."

2. _____

3. _____

4. _____

5. _____

6. _____

7. _____

(Endnotes)

i   Martin Meredith, *The Fortunes of Africa,* Simon & Schuster, London, 2014

ii Conflicts in Africa; *Jewish World Watch;* International Association of Genocide Scholars; BBC; Kenya Human Rights Commission

iii New Bible Dictionary, Inter-Varsity Press, Leicester, England/ Illinois, USA, 1982

iv The NIV Study Bible, notes on Genesis 2:13. The Zondervan Corporation, 1985

CHAPTER THREE

Plague of Frogs (Witchcraft & Idolatry)

Pharaonic Confrontation:

Exodus 8:1-15 And the Lord spoke to Moses, "Go to Pharaoh and say to him, 'Thus says the Lord: "Let My people go, that they may serve Me. *Plague of Frogs (Witchcraft & Idolatry)* ² But if you refuse to let *them* go, behold, I will smite all your territory with frogs. ³ So the river shall bring forth frogs abundantly, which shall go up and come into your house, into your bedroom, on your bed, into the houses of your servants, on your people, into your ovens, and into your kneading bowls. ⁴ And the frogs shall come up on you, on your people, and on all your servants."'" ⁵ Then the Lord spoke to Moses, "Say to Aaron, 'Stretch out your hand with your rod over the streams, over the rivers, and over the ponds, and cause frogs to come up on the land of Egypt.'" ⁶ So Aaron stretched out his hand over the waters of Egypt, and the frogs came up and covered the land of Egypt. ⁷ And the magicians did so with their enchantments, and brought up frogs on the land of Egypt.

[8] Then Pharaoh called for Moses and Aaron, and said, "Entreat the LORD that He may take away the frogs from me and from my people; and I will let the people go, that they may sacrifice to the LORD." [9] And Moses said to Pharaoh, "Accept the honor of saying when I shall intercede for you, for your servants, and for your people, to destroy the frogs from you and your houses, *that* they may remain in the river only." [10] So he said, "Tomorrow." And he said, "*Let it be* according to your word, that you may know that *there is* no one like the LORD OUR GOD. [11] And the frogs shall depart from you, from your houses, from your servants, and from your people. They shall remain in the river only."

[12] Then Moses and Aaron went out from Pharaoh. And Moses cried out to the LORD concerning the frogs which He had brought against Pharaoh. [13] So the LORD did according to the word of Moses. And the frogs died out of the houses, out of the courtyards, and out of the fields. [14] They gathered them together in heaps, and the land stank. [15] But when Pharaoh saw that there was relief, he hardened his heart and did not heed them, as the LORD had said.

Post-Exodus Judgment:

Isaiah 19:3 "The Egyptians will lose heart, and I will bring their plans to nothing; they will consult the idols and the spirits of the dead, the mediums and the spiritists."

Snapshot: (Abomination across the Continent)

In September 2016, the South African minister for Higher Education, Blade Nzimande, announced that universities in South Africa were now allowed to offer BSc. degree in Witchcraft. "I think this is a good idea. We have agreed that from next year, 2018, all universities will be allowed to offer BSc. in Witchcraft. After consultations, we unanimously agreed to incorporate the program into the curriculum".[i]

During the war in Congo in the 1990s, a soothsayer announced that you could be cured of HIV if you ate a pygmy. Not long afterwards, evidence was that in Pygmy village several men had "disappeared" as a result.[ii]

Albinos live in constant mortal fear, particularly in Tanzania, Burundi, Malawi and Zambia. Albinos are widely persecuted by witch doctors who believe their body parts bring wealth and good luck. Every year albino children are kidnapped and have their limbs, hair, teeth and even genitals hacked off with machetes to be used in good luck potions which are then sold at a premium.

Child sacrifice is rampant in Uganda, where those looking for financial and political fortune resort to kidnapping children and bringing their blood and body parts to be consumed by spirits. It is coming out of a revanchist spirit that has brought back traditional leadership whose foundations are in idolatry.

In South Africa the writer V.S. Naipaul noted that human body parts were made by witch doctors into a mixture of so-called battle medicine for respectable middle-class Africans.

A number of African leaders are reputed to be cannibalistic presidents. Leaders in Equatorial Guinea and the Central African Republic were reputed cannibals.

Witchcraft and sorcery are the result of the desire to control resources. Most Africans have grown up in dire poverty, be it in rural or urban settings. In the villages sorcery is usually about prosperity; trade and business in urban centres is ridden with witchcraft. It is normal for big business to be sold out to Free Masonry and other divinations, including Eastern religion and mysticism.

Fact:

In 2010, V.S. Naipaul, the Trinidadian writer and Nobel laureate, published a book, 'The Masque of Africa: Glimpses of African Belief' in which he describes ancestor worship, child sacrifice, witch doctors, totemism, pagan initiation rights, necromancy, and a whole range of acts and actions emanating from idolatry on the continent. Naipaul lived in Uganda for a while in the 1960s, and returned there in the 2000s at the start of a six-month journey that took him into the spirit world of Nigeria, Gabon, Ivory Coast, Ghana, and South Africa. In each country he asked questions, listened attentively and noticed, as he chronicled African beliefs, societies that are so deeply entrenched in witchcraft and idolatry.

The African Renaissance, spearheaded by South Africa, is advocating the return to the worship of ancestral spirits[iii], which is idolatry. It is a philosophy that has particularly appealed to politicians, who find it convenient to identify Christianity with colonial rule and Apartheid.

Witchcraft seats comfortably in the mainstream of many African societies. It is available on satellite television in 'Africa Magic', a channel that airs across the continent; in movies of the ascendant Nigerian film industry Nollywood; in football stadia; and at political rallies.

Prophetic Implication:

Revelation 16:13 says, "And I saw three evil spirits that looked like frogs leap from the mouths of the dragon, the beast, and the false prophet."

When the plague broke out (Exodus 8:3-4), frogs filled the Nile, the palaces (State Houses), Pharaoh's bed (representing the innermost place of his rulership), officials' houses (Government offices are replete with witchcraft), the people (general citizenry of a nation), ovens (manufacturing enterprises/business paces), and kneading troughs (livelihood). This is what has been happening in African life: witchcraft and idolatry are so pervasive they are in corridors of power, in communities, in the economy.

The magicians were at home replicating this (8:7). In the same way that non-believer Presidents coral Christian pastors to pray for them and their offices regularly without taking that all-important step of surrendering to Christ, so did the Pharaoh ask for intercession (8:8).

It is said that one of the physio-spiritual characters of witchcraft is that it has an unnatural stench, as did the pile of dead frogs (8:14). Witchcraft defiles the land.

God's Principle:

There are only two sources of spiritual power: God and Satan. Satan has only the power that God allows him to have, but it is considerable (Job 1:12; 2 Corinthians 4:4; Revelation 20:2). To seek spirituality, knowledge, or power apart from God is idolatry.

Witchcraft is Satan's realm, and he excels in counterfeiting what God does, the same way the magicians in Pharaoh's court did. At the heart of witchcraft is the desire to know the future and control events that are not ours to control. Those abilities belong only to the Lord. This desire has its roots in Satan's first temptation to Eve: "You can be like God" (Genesis 3:5).[iv]

Deuteronomy 18:9-12 says, "When you enter the land the Lord your God is giving you, do not learn to imitate the detestable ways of the nations there. Let no one be found among you who sacrifices their son or daughter in the fire, who practices divination or sorcery, interprets omens, engages in witchcraft, or casts spells, or who is a medium or spiritist or who consults the dead. Anyone who does these things is detestable to the Lord."

"When someone tells you to consult mediums and spiritists, who whisper and mutter, should not a people inquire of their God? Why consult the dead on behalf of the living?" (Isaiah 8:19)

"Do not permit any of your children to be offered as a sacrifice to Molech, for you must not bring shame on the name of your God. I am the LORD." (Leviticus 18:21)

<u>Prayer Points:</u>

1. Repentance

2. _____

3. _____

4. _____

5. _____

6. _____

7. _____

(End Notes)

i   Venas News Kenya

ii   Johann Hari, *The Valley of Taboos* http://www.slate.com/articles/arts/books/2010/10/the_valley_of_taboos.html

iii   Laban Jjumba, *Four Giants Confronting Africa.* Beeranga Mwesigwa Foundation, Kampala, 2016

iv   Got Questions.org

CHAPTER FOUR

Plague of Gnats/Lice (Tribalism & Nepotism)

Pharaonic Confrontation:

Exodus 8:16-19 ¹⁶ Then the LORD said to Moses, "Tell Aaron, 'Stretch out your staff and strike the dust of the ground,' and throughout the land of Egypt the dust will become gnats." ¹⁷ They did this, and when Aaron stretched out his hand with the staff and struck the dust of the ground, gnats came on people and animals. All the dust throughout the land of Egypt became gnats. ¹⁸ But when the magicians tried to produce gnats by their secret arts, they could not.

Since the gnats were on people and animals everywhere, ¹⁹ the magicians said to Pharaoh, "This is the finger of God." But Pharaoh's heart was hard and he would not listen, just as the LORD had said.

Post-Exodus Judgment:

Isaiah 19:4 "I will hand the Egyptians over to the power of a cruel master, and a fierce king will rule over them," declares the Lord, the LORD Almighty.

Snapshot: (The Bane of Africa)

A tribe is an ethnic group that shares common history, culture and nature. Dictatorships in Africa have mostly been held together by the glue of tribalism and nepotism. Africa has over 3,000 tribes, and each has an interest in economic livelihood. Because the economies are not advanced, the surest way of accessing livelihood comes through control of political power which, in turn, is allegiant to nepotism which then kicks off a vicious cycle. At Independence, whereas most politicians came in with nationalist credentials, they steadily came to rely on ethnic support as the main political base. In exploiting this base, there emerged a ruthlessness that has resulted in cruel rule, first with military dictatorships but eventually even with the façade of elections. As long as there is no class formation that allows the emergence of democratic rule, the tribal factor continues to be central in governance.

Among the 3,000 tribes are 2,000 languages, which many times are abused and used to advance ethnocentrism.

Ethnocentrism in Africa exists alongside nepotism, the practice among those with power or influence of favouring relatives or friends, especially by giving them jobs. During his rule from 1970 to 1980, Liberian President William Tolbert had his brother Stephen A. Tolbert serving as his finance minister and another brother, Frank E. Tolbert as President Pro-Tempore of the Senate (equivalent of Speaker of Parliament). Tolbert's daughter Wokie had married a son of former President Tubman, who Tolbert served as Vice President for close to 20 years before succeeding him. In the mid-1970s several Cabinet members belonged to the Tolbert-clan.

The cruel masters of Isaiah 19:4, who rule over Africa, are partly responsible for the ethnocentricity. The leaders of Africa have been despotic. From the pre-colonial kings and chiefs, to the colonial enforcers, to the post-Independence nationalists to the military dictators who replaced them on to the post-Cold War set that has used the veneer of elections and new constitutions to disguise autocratic tendencies, Africa has been dealt a cruel hand, as Scripture prophesied.

Fact:

Reason Wafawarova, a Zimbabwean, has dissected tribalism in Africa: "Tribalism is the symbol of Africa's divided soul. Tribalism is the clash between peace and unrest, the clash between unity and division, the divide between tribe and nation, the clash between tradition and change, the bane between fact and aspiration, and indeed it is the clash between politics and rationality."[i]

The 20 most ethnically diverse countries in the world are all on the African continent. Nigeria has 250 ethnic groups or tribes, including the three big ones - Hausa-Fulani (29% of the population), Yoruba (21%) and Igbo, or Ibo (18%). Uganda and Kenya also have wide ethnic diversity, Kenya boasting more than 70 ethnic groups and Uganda registering at least 40 distinct ethnicities. In the Kenyan capital Nairobi, even the slums, particularly the 2,500,000-strong Kibera is chopped up in tribal villages. As if the poverty and deprivation of slum life were not enough, the plague of tribal division is thrown into the miserable mix.

'It is Our Turn to Eat' is the title of a non-fiction political thriller on the scourge of tribalism and nepotism in

Kenya and beyond by the British author Michela Wrong. It is also a well-used phrase for those looking to put their snouts in the trough of Africa's politics and economies – in Uganda, this world view has been heard being applied as "*twarire*" ("we have eaten") by one ethnic community, while another group has been known to clamour for "*ebyaffe*" ("our things") from the national heritage.

After long-awaited, long fought-for Independence from domination by the Arab north from 1955 to 2005, South Sudan promptly broke up into ethno-centred violence, enjoying barely four years of hard-won Independence. The few years of self-rule have been punctuated with bouts of ethnic cleansing and the odd massacre of targeted communities.

Prophetic Implication:

Gnats and (or) lice are found everywhere in the world, just as ethnic groupings are. Gnats/lice need the blood of warm-blooded hosts to survive. African politics and the socio-economic setup are heavily dependent on blood and ethnic connections. Gnats are tiny creatures, no bigger than the head of a pin – African tribes are, in the main, tiny and unviable on their own. And so using an ethno-centric approach to the management of national affairs, like economic opportunity, job allocations, and resource mobilisation, is not tenable, as it simply sucks the blood out of systems and institutions.

Pharaoh's magicians tried to replicate the plague of gnats but they did not succeed (Exodus 8:18). In frustration, they gave up, declaring to Pharaoh, "This is the Finger of God" (8:19). The reason they could not duplicate this was that *man was created by God in His Image*. This will not be done/copied by the enemy since man is God's highest creation (Genesis 1:26-28).

The finger represents the highest and most delicate of artistic applications – painters, guitarists/harpists/violinists, drummers, surgeons, others – all use fingers. Similarly God's creative work (Psalm 8:3) of the physical world and, most of all deliverance from demons and evil power (Luke 11:20) [which, actually, is the main reason Jesus came] were delivered by His Finger. It is God Who placed man in the ethnic groupings, and Satan cannot copy that. Satan can only corrupt it, so the magicians could not replicate.

God's Principle:

"There is neither Greek nor Jew....for you are all one in Christ Jesus. If you belong to Christ, then you are Abraham's seed, and heirs according to the promise." (Galatians 3:28-29)

"I will make you into a great nation .... and all peoples on earth will be blessed through you" (Genesis 12:2/3). God's promise to Abraham has a sevenfold structure:

a. I will make you into a great nation

b. I will bless you

c. I will make your name great

d. You will be a blessing

e. I will bless those who bless you

f. Whoever curses you I will curse

g. All peoples on earth will be blessed through you.

<u>Prayer Points:</u>

1. Repentance

2. _____

3. _____

4. _____

5. _____

6. _____

7. _____

(Endnotes)

i   New Zimbabwe, Harare, 5 August 2015

CHAPTER FIVE

Plague of Flies (Sanitation & Slums)

Pharaonic Confrontation:

Exodus 8:20-32 Then the LORD said to Moses, "Get up early in the morning and confront Pharaoh as he goes to the water and say to him, 'This is what the LORD says: Let my people go, so that they may worship me. If you do not let my people go, I will send swarms of flies on you and your officials, on your people and into your houses. The houses of the Egyptians will be full of flies, and even the ground where they are. "'But on that day I will deal differently with the land of Goshen, where my people live; no swarms of flies will be there, so that you will know that I, the LORD, am in this land. I will make a distinction between my people and your people. This miraculous sign will occur tomorrow.'"

And the LORD did this. Dense swarms of flies poured into Pharaoh's palace and into the houses of his officials, and throughout Egypt the land was ruined by the flies. Then Pharaoh summoned Moses and Aaron and said, "Go, sacrifice to your God here in the land." But Moses said, "That would not be right. The sacrifices we offer the

LORD our God would be detestable to the Egyptians. And if we offer sacrifices that are detestable in their eyes, will they not stone us? We must take a three-day journey into the desert to offer sacrifices to the LORD our God, as he commands us." Pharaoh said, "I will let you go to offer sacrifices to the LORD your God in the desert, but you must not go very far. Now pray for me." Moses answered, "As soon as I leave you, I will pray to the LORD, and tomorrow the flies will leave Pharaoh and his officials and his people. Only be sure that Pharaoh does not act deceitfully again by not letting the people go to offer sacrifices to the LORD."

Then Moses left Pharaoh and prayed to the LORD, and the LORD did what Moses asked: The flies left Pharaoh and his officials and his people; not a fly remained. But this time also Pharaoh hardened his heart and would not let the people go.

Post-Exodus Judgment:

Isaiah 19:6 "The canals will stink."

Snapshot: (Urban Squalor)

Sixty per cent of Africans still live in rural places[i], whereas more than 70% of people in Latin America, North America and Europe live in cities[ii]. Urbanisation is, on the whole, considered to be central to the advancement of human society. While 60% of people in Sub-Saharan Africa still live in rural areas, Africa is the fastest urbanising region of the world. The United Nations projects that by 2030 Africa will be a predominantly urban continent. Urbanisation is due in part to rural-to-urban migration, in part to natural increase, and in part due to the reclassification of urban boundaries as cities expand outwards and small population centres grow and are designated as urban areas.

But the mode in which Africa is urbanising is not healthy because more than 60% of urbanised Africans live in slums and do not have adequate access to safe water, sanitation and other infrastructure. Slum life in Africa is a cesspool of disease, pestilence and sickness, which in the physical is manifested in the form of great numbers of flies. Typhoid, cholera, dysentery, and malaria break out commonly in the slums.

Unclean water and poor sanitation are a leading cause of child mortality. An estimated 800 children die every day from diarrhoea, spread through poor sanitation and hygiene. Forty per cent of the world's population, around 3 billion people, lacks access to toilets. All seven continents are affected, although South Asia and Sub-Saharan Africa are the worst off.

In Botswana, one of the more prosperous countries of Southern Africa, over 90% of the population has access to safe drinking water, but only 60% has improved sanitation. In rural areas, that drops to 40%. In Kenya over half the population has clean drinking water, but only a third is covered by sanitation programmes. In rural regions of arid West African countries like Chad, Niger and Mauritania, less than 10% of the population has toilets.[iii]

Africa's 20 Worst Slums[iv]:

20. Ezbet el-Haggana (Egypt): Located in Cairo, has population of more than one million

19. Alexandra, Gauteng (South Africa): Part of city of

Johannesburg, has more than 20,000 informal dwellings or shacks

18. Nima Slum (Ghana): Part of Greater Accra, has very poor sanitation facilities

17. Kennedy Road (South Africa): Part of port city of Durban, it has poor infrastructure

16. Cazenga (Angola): Part of Luanda, houses 425,000 people in deplorable conditions

15. Ajegunle (Nigeria): In the heart of Lagos, poorest and toughest neighbourhood

14. Mukuru kwa Njenga (Kenya): In East Nairobi, many of its 100,000 population died of cholera in 2009

13. Shomolu (Nigeria): In Ikeja, Lagos, it has horrible infrastructure

12. Kangemi (Kenya): Housing more than 100,000 on the outskirts of Nairobi, it has no sewerage system

11. Ilaje: (Nigeria): Built in Lagos Lagoon

10. Clara Town (Liberia): It is a swamp in Barshod Island, Monrovia, and is flooded most of the time

9. Agbogbloshie (Ghana): Located in South Ghana, it has been labelled the world's largest waste-dumping site. It is commonly known as Sodom & Gomorrah. Say no more

8. Kiambiu (Kenya): 50,000 residents in this Nairobi slum

7. Kawangware (Kenya): 15km west of Nairobi city centre, houses hundreds of thousands

6. Korogocho (Kenya): 200,000 on outskirts of Nairobi

5. Makoko (Nigeria): In Lagos Lagoon, people navigate around on stilts

4. West Point (Liberia): In Monrovia, on a peninsula that juts into Atlantic Ocean, tuberculosis has killed many

3. Mathare (Kenya): Outside Nairobi, it is a collection of slums where 500,000 people live

2. Kroo Bay (Sierra Leone): Sprawling in Freetown. Over 95% of houses do not have a toilet, so river carries human waste

1. Kibera (Kenya): Outside of Nairobi, it is the largest urban slum in Africa, housing about 2.5 million people, or half of Nairobi's population. Kibera has villages that have a tribal character, adding one plague to another.

Fact:

A 'kabaka' (king) of Buganda, a pre-existent kingdom in Uganda, was touring his realm when one of the bearers of his portable royal throne stepped in human waste that had been dropped by a child in the homestead the monarch was to rest in. Flustered, the king (who oral history says was either the 12th, Kabaka Sekamanya, 1487-1517, or the 13th, Kabaka Kimbugwe, 1517-1547), decreed that forthwith all homesteads were to have properly constructed latrines and sanitation would become a public health priority.

What went wrong in Uganda in the intervening years, between 1500 and now? The country's sanitation seems to have taken a backward step from when that royal decree was pronounced half a millennium ago. Slums in Kenya and Uganda have a waste disposal phenomenon known as "flying toilets", which means that human waste is packed in a polythene bag which is then discarded wantonly, sometimes over the heads, or onto the feet, of passers-by. Toilets are not as common as assumed in Africa.

In 2006, 38% of the population in Africa used an improved sanitation facility - an increase from 33% in 1990. Less than a third of the African rural population, and just over half of the urban population used improved sanitation. In 16 of the 54 African countries less than 25% of the population uses an improved sanitation facility. Africa as a continent did not meet the MDG sanitation target. Only five of the 54 countries were on track to meet that particular Millennium Development Goal, one of the United Nations-determined targets for addressing extreme poverty in its many dimensions of income poverty, hunger, disease, lack of adequate shelter, and exclusion by the time the deadline came at the end of 2015.

A documentary on the BBC World Service in February 2015 lauded the athletic talent replete in Africa when featuring Ivorian champion sprinter Murielle Ahoure. Describing a state-of-the-art training facility in Yamoussoukro, Ivory Coast, the programme nevertheless described the place as being filthy with rubbish. Most African townships and trading centres on highways are flyblown. Garbage collection in the cities leaves a lot to be desired. Many hospitals and health centres lack the antiseptic cleanliness that is foundational to the physical healing process. Alongside flies, the ghettos and tenements of Africa are infested with rats and cockroaches.

Prophetic Implication:

In prophetic language, flies are representative of evil[v]. They are the results of unclean actions.

God's Principle:

"Designate a place outside the camp where you can go to relieve yourself. As part of your equipment have something to dig with, and when you relieve yourself, dig a hole and cover up your excrement." Deuteronomy 23:12-13

"The one to be cleansed shall then wash his clothes and shave off all his hair and bathe in water and be clean. Now afterward, he may enter the camp, but he shall stay outside his tent for seven days." Leviticus 14:8

"The acts of the sinful nature are obvious: sexual immorality, impurity and sensuality." Galatians 5:19

"I appeal to you therefore, brothers, by the mercies of God, to present your bodies as a living sacrifice, holy and acceptable to God, which is your spiritual worship." Romans 12:1

"For you were bought with a price. So glorify God in your body." 1 Corinthians 6:20

Prayer Points:

1. Repentance

2. _____

3. _____

4. _____

5. _____

6. _____

7. _____

(Endnotes)

i   World Bank

ii   World Bank Urbanization and Rural - Urban Welfare Inequalities

iii   World Press

iv   Africa Ranking

v   Joe Ibojie, *Bible-based Dictionary of Prophetic Symbols for Every Christian.* Cross House Books, Aberdeen, 2009

CHAPTER SIX

Plague *on* Livestock (Poverty)

Pharaonic Confrontation:

Exodus 9:1-7 Then the LORD said to Moses, "Go to Pharaoh and say to him, 'This is what the LORD, the God of the Hebrews, says: "Let my people go, so that they may worship me." If you refuse to let them go and continue to hold them back, the hand of the LORD will bring a terrible plague on your livestock in the field—on your horses and donkeys and camels and on your cattle and sheep and goats. But the LORD will make a distinction between the livestock of Israel and that of Egypt, so that no animal belonging to the Israelites will die.' " The LORD set a time and said, "Tomorrow the LORD will do this in the land."

And the next day the LORD did it: All the livestock of the Egyptians died, but not one animal belonging to the Israelites died. Pharaoh sent men to investigate and found that not even one of the animals of the Israelites had died. Yet his heart was unyielding and he would not let the people go.

Post-Exodus Judgment:

Isaiah 19:8-9 "The fishermen will groan and lament, all who cast hooks into the Nile; those who throw nets on the water will pine away. Those who work with combed flax will despair, the weavers of fine linen will lose hope."

Snapshot: (Widespread Impoverishment)

- Seventy-five per cent of the world's poorest countries are located in Africa

- According to Gallup World, in 2013, the 10 countries with the highest proportion of residents living in extreme poverty were all in sub-Saharan Africa

- Approximately one in three people living in sub-Saharan Africa are undernourished. The Food and Agriculture Organization (FAO) of the United Nations estimated that 239 million people (around 30% of the population) in sub-Saharan Africa went hungry in 2010

- In sub-Saharan Africa, 589 million people live without electricity. As a result, a staggering 80% of the population relies on biomass products such as wood, charcoal and dung in order to cook

- Of the 738 million people globally who lack access to clean water, 37% are living in sub-Saharan Africa. Poverty in Africa results in over 500 million people suffering from waterborne diseases[i]

Poorest Countries in Africa

12. Mali – GDP per capita $715

11. Sierra Leone - GDP per capita $679

10. Togo - GDP per capita $636

9. Eritrea - GDP per capita $544

8. Ethiopia - GDP per capita $505

7. DR Congo - GDP per capita $484

6. Madagascar - GDP per capita $463

5. Liberia - GDP per capita $454

4. Niger - GDP per capita $415

3. Central African Republic - GDP per capita $333

2. Burundi - GDP per capita $267

1. Malawi - GDP per capita $226[ii]

Fact:

Decade after decade, politicians and international organisations have failed to tackle poverty in Africa. Nor have they been able to help generate growth or build sufficient basic infrastructure. Between 1975 and 2000 Africa was the only place on earth where poverty intensified.[iii] Since then things have been changing but some countries still struggle more than others.

Poverty across the continent may be lower than what current estimates suggest, though the number of people living in extreme poverty has grown substantially since

1990, according to the World Bank Africa poverty report 'Poverty in a Rising Africa, 2016'. The share of Africans who are in extreme poverty fell from 56% in 1990 to 43% in 2012, but because of population growth many more people are poor, the report said. The most optimistic scenario shows about 330 million poor in 2012, up from about 280 million in 1990. Poverty reduction has been slowest in fragile countries.[iv]

Prophetic Implication:

Livestock is livelihood, which is the economy. When the fifth plague was pronounced, unlike the others that were *OF* one nature or other, this one was *ON* the livestock, which in the agrarian setting of Ancient Egypt meant the economy. Many African countries are aid-dependent for budget support, since they are unable to raise sufficient internal revenue. This, in turn, renders them indebted, which then affects their ability to pay debts and increases their debt-service ratio, which then eats into their export earnings. They are exporters of low value primary products and importers of high value technologies, which then unbalances their terms of trade and exacerbates their poverty.

God's Principle:

1. The Importance of Work: Work is simultaneously an aspect of the image of God and the normal means God gives us to provide for our needs and for the needs of others. Scripture tells us we should all be seeking to work rather than to live off the generosity of others.

2. The Importance of Moral Proximity: We have responsibilities to others in proportion to our

relationship with them: those who are closer to us have more of a claim on us that those who are distant. Proximity is determined by relationships rather than geography. Moral proximity looks at problems and asks, "Where am I personally responsible to act given my finite time and resources?"

3. The Importance of Subsidiarity Proximity: Argues that solutions are best found on as local a level as possible, and looks at problems and asks who is best-equipped to deal with them. Using either principle 2 or 3, the process begins with the family. In accordance with moral proximity, Jesus understood the commandment, "Honour your father and mother," to mean that we need to provide for our parents even ahead of giving to the Temple (Mark 7:9-13). Further, Paul tells us that we are responsible to take care of our grandparents rather than passing them off to the Church (or to the government) to take care of them (1 Timothy 5:4). Subsidiarity states that if the family cannot solve the problem, friends, community groups, and churches should step in. Only after these private agencies are exhausted should the problem move to government or foreign bodies like NGOs, bilateral or multilateral partners, and then once again on as local a level as possible. This is where the biblical approach to poverty relief flies in the face of what is done commonly.

4. The Importance of Giving: All of these principles mean nothing unless we follow biblical teaching about the importance of giving generously and even sacrificially to those in need. "If a brother or

sister is poorly clothed and lacking in daily food, and one of you says to them, 'Go in peace, be warmed and filled,' without giving them the things needed for the body, what good is that?" (James 2:15-16) "If anyone has this world's goods and sees his brother in need, yet closes his heart against him, how does God's love abide in him?"[v]

Practical Issues

- **Poverty alleviation is the church's responsibility**. It is the job of the church, the body of Christ, to care passionately and genuinely for the poor. The church must step up to their responsibility and be the first line of offense in addressing poverty.

- **When we do what God has created us to do, we help others**. The impact of our work extends to God's kingdom in ways we will never understand. Embrace volunteer opportunities. Serve your church. Work hard at your job every day. Love your family, friends, and neighbours well.

- **The fight to end poverty starts in your community**. It starts with building long-term relationships, getting your hands dirty, and addressing real needs.[vi]

Prayer Points:

1. Repentance

2. _____

3. _____

4. _____

5. _____

6. _____

7. _____

(Endnotes)

i   The Borgen Project

ii   AnswersAfrica

iii   Poverties

iv   World Bank Poverty in a Rising Africa report

v   Institute for Faith, Work & Economics

vi   Christianity Today, October 2015

CHAPTER SEVEN

Plague of Boils (Disease & Epidemics)

Pharaonic Confrontation:

Exodus 9:8-12 Then the LORD said to Moses and Aaron, "Take handfuls of soot from a furnace and have Moses toss it into the air in the presence of Pharaoh. It will become fine dust over the whole land of Egypt, and festering boils will break out on men and animals throughout the land." So they took soot from a furnace and stood before Pharaoh. Moses tossed it into the air, and festering boils broke out on men and animals. The magicians could not stand before Moses because of the boils that were on them and on all the Egyptians. But the LORD hardened Pharaoh's heart and he would not listen to Moses and Aaron, just as the LORD had said to Moses.

Post-Exodus Judgment:

Isaiah 19:10 "The workers in cloth will be dejected, and all the wage earners will be sick at heart."

Snapshot: (Africa more prone)

Epidemic and pandemic-prone diseases threaten public health security. These include diseases such as cholera, meningitis, avian influenza, and viral haemorrhagic fevers for which the Africa region reports considerably high incidence and mortality rates. They can be responsible for high levels of disease and death and have a devastating impact on the economies of the region.[i]

Countries in the WHO African Region continue to be affected by recurring epidemics of cholera, malaria, meningitis, measles and zoonotic diseases including viral haemorrhagic fevers, plague and dengue fever. The epidemics significantly impact on health and economic development in the Region.[ii] Conditions favouring recurring epidemics are prevalent in most African states. Inadequate access to safe water and sanitation, underlying health conditions, limited public awareness of prevailing health risks, and weak health systems with limited capacity for timely identification and response to epidemics all contribute to the frequency and severity of epidemics.

Epidemics associated with high morbidity and mortality often occur over large geographical areas. Between 2004 and 2008, 13 countries reported a total of 170,927 meningitis cases, 44 countries reported a total of 749,713 measles cases, and 41 countries reported a total of 691,290 cholera cases. Recurring epidemics of cholera, meningitis and measles were reported by numerous countries.[iii]

Case fatality ratios (CFRs) reached 5% or higher during some cholera outbreaks, 10% or higher during some meningitis epidemics, and 60% or higher during most Ebola and Marburg outbreaks. In 2009, all 46 sub-Saharan Africa states reported at least one disease epidemic: 33 countries reported pandemic influenza A

(H1N1), 20 countries reported cholera, seven countries reported meningitis, and Malawi and Mozambique reported typhoid. The meningitis belt stretches over 21 countries (Cape Verde-Senegal-Gambia-Guinea Bissau-Mauritania-Guinea-Mali-Burkina Faso-Ivory Coast-Ghana-Togo-Benin-Nigeria-Niger-Chad-Sao Tome & Principe-Cameroon- Central African Republic-Sudan-South Sudan-Uganda-Kenya-Ethiopia-Eritrea) with a total of 495 million inhabitants at high risk of epidemic during the meningitis season (October to May). During the meningitis 2009 season, 81,283 cases and 4473 deaths (CFR = 5.5%) were reported by 14 countries in the meningitis belt.

Fact:

When the Ebola outbreak hit West Africa in 2014-15, some 11,325 out of 28,652 cases (Suspected, Probable, and Confirmed)[iv] died, a mortality rate of two out of five people. Meanwhile, all infected persons flown overseas made a full recovery except one man, who died in the US.

In 2007, African countries experienced economic losses of US$ 60 million as a result of cholera.

Sub-Saharan Africa has the most serious HIV and AIDS epidemic in the world. In 2013, an estimated 24.7 million people were living with HIV, accounting for 71% of the global total. In the same year, there were an estimated 1.5 million new HIV infections and 1.1 million AIDS-related deaths.[v]

Prophetic Implication:

Of the ten plagues, the Plague of Boils is one of only three that were not announced to Pharaoh (the other two being Gnats and Darkness). This is because disease tends to strike communities and nations unannounced, unlike war/bloodshed, or idolatry or famine or poverty, which can be seen coming.

God's Principle:

"The Lord will strike you with wasting disease, with fever and inflammation...which will plague you until you perish" (Deuteronomy 28:22).

"Whoever touches the dead body of anyone and fails to purify himself defiles the LORD'S tabernacle. That person must be cut off from Israel. Because the water of cleansing has not been sprinkled on him, he is unclean; his uncleanness remains on him. "This is the law that applies when a person dies in a tent: Anyone who enters the tent and anyone who is in it will be unclean for seven days, and every open container without a lid fastened on it will be unclean. "Anyone out in the open who touches someone who has been killed with a sword or someone who has died a natural death, or anyone who touches a human bone or a grave, will be unclean for seven days. "For the unclean person, put some ashes from the burned purification offering into a jar and pour fresh water over them. Then a man who is ceremonially clean is to take some hyssop, dip it in the water and sprinkle the tent and all the furnishings and the people who were there. He must also sprinkle anyone who has touched a human bone or a grave or someone who has been killed or someone who has died a natural death. The man who is clean is to sprinkle the unclean person on the third and seventh days, and on the seventh day he is to purify him. The person being cleansed must wash his clothes and bathe with water, and that evening he will be clean." (Numbers 19:13-19)

Jesus healed "every disease and every sickness," as well as plagues in the areas He visited (Matthew 9:35; 10:1; Mark 3:10). Just as God chose to use plagues and disease to show His power to the Israelites, Jesus healed as an exhibition of the same power to verify that He was truly the Son of God. He gave the same healing power to the disciples to verify their ministry (Luke 9:1). God still allows sickness for His own purposes, but sometimes disease, even worldwide pandemics, are simply the result of living in a fallen world.

We need to exercise greater personal responsibility over the lifestyle choices that impact our health: our diet, our emotional well-being, our relationships with others, our hygiene, our environment. God's Word provides guidance in all these areas. The immune system designed by God will function effectively when we pay attention to all these areas.

Prayer Points:

    1.   Repentance

    2.   _____

    3.   _____

    4.   _____

    5.   _____

    6.   _____

    7.   _____

(Endnotes)

i   World Health Organization Regional Office for Africa

ii African Health Observatory, World Health Organization

iii Ibid.

iv Centers for Disease Control and Prevention

v AVERT

CHAPTER EIGHT

Plague of Hail
(Drought, Famine, Ecology)

Pharaonic Confrontation:

Exodus 9:13-35 ¹³ Then the LORD said to Moses, "Rise early in the morning and stand before Pharaoh, and say to him, 'Thus says the LORD God of the Hebrews: "Let My people go, that they may serve Me, ¹⁴ for at this time I will send all My plagues to your very heart, and on your servants and on your people, that you may know that *there is* none like Me in all the earth. ¹⁵ Now if I had stretched out My hand and struck you and your people with pestilence, then you would have been cut off from the earth. ¹⁶ But indeed for this *purpose* I have raised you up, that I may show My power *in* you, and that My name may be declared in all the earth. ¹⁷ As yet you exalt yourself against My people in that you will not let them go. ¹⁸ Behold, tomorrow about this time I will cause very heavy hail to rain down, such as has not been in Egypt since its founding until now. ¹⁹ Therefore send now *and* gather your livestock and all that you have in the field, for the hail shall come down on every man and every animal which is found in the field and is not brought home; and they shall die." ' "

²⁰ He who feared the word of the LORD among the servants of Pharaoh made his servants and his livestock flee to the houses. ²¹ But he who did not regard the word of the LORD left his servants and his livestock in the field.

²² Then the LORD said to Moses, "Stretch out your hand toward heaven, that there may be hail in all the land of Egypt—on man, on beast, and on every herb of the field, throughout the land of Egypt." ²³ And Moses stretched out his rod toward heaven; and the LORD sent thunder and hail, and fire darted to the ground. And the Lord rained hail on the land of Egypt. ²⁴ So there was hail, and fire mingled with the hail, so very heavy that there was none like it in all the land of Egypt since it became a nation. ²⁵ And the hail struck throughout the whole land of Egypt, all that *was* in the field, both man and beast; and the hail struck every herb of the field and broke every tree of the field. ²⁶ Only in the land of Goshen, where the children of Israel *were,* there was no hail.

²⁷ And Pharaoh sent and called for Moses and Aaron, and said to them, "I have sinned this time. The LORD *is* righteous, and my people and I *are* wicked. ²⁸ Entreat the LORD, that there may be no *more* mighty thundering and hail, for *it is* enough. I will let you go, and you shall stay no longer."

²⁹ So Moses said to him, "As soon as I have gone out of the city, I will spread out my hands to the LORD; the thunder will cease, and there will be no more hail, that you may know that the earth *is* the LORD'S. ³⁰ But as for you and your servants, I know that you will not yet fear the LORD God."

[31] Now the flax and the barley were struck, for the barley *was* in the head and the flax *was* in bud. [32] But the wheat and the spelt were not struck, for they *are* late crops.

[33] So Moses went out of the city from Pharaoh and spread out his hands to the LORD; then the thunder and the hail ceased, and the rain was not poured on the earth. [34] And when Pharaoh saw that the rain, the hail, and the thunder had ceased, he sinned yet more; and he hardened his heart, he and his servants. [35] So the heart of Pharaoh was hard; neither would he let the children of Israel go, as the LORD had spoken by Moses.

Post-Exodus Judgment:

Isaiah 19:6b-7 "The streams of Egypt will dwindle and dry up. The reeds and rushes will wither, also the plants along the Nile, at the mouth of the river. Every sown field along the Nile will become parched, will blow away and be no more."

Snapshot: (Disaster Comes in Cycles)

In 1985, Ethiopia suffered what was assumed to be the last of the large-scale famines affecting many millions. Not so. In 2016 countries were just waking up to the most serious global food crisis of quarter of a century caused by the strongest El Nino weather event since 1982, droughts and heat-waves ravaged much of India, Latin America and parts of south-east Asia. But the worst effects of this natural phenomenon, which begins with waters warming in the equatorial Pacific, are to be found in southern Africa. Three consecutive years without rain were threatening catastrophe for some of the poorest people in the world.[i] Malawi, Mozambique, Lesotho, Zimbabwe, Namibia, Madagascar, Angola and Swaziland declared national emergencies or disasters, as did seven of South Africa's nine provinces. Other countries, including Botswana and the Democratic Republic of the Congo, were also badly hit.

By Christmas 2016, around 49 million people across almost all of southern Africa needed food aid. With 12 million more hungry people in Ethiopia, 6 million in Southern Sudan and more in the Central African Republic and Chad, a continent-scale food crisis was unfolding.

In January 2017, legislators were urging the Kenyan government to declare drought in North Rift region a national disaster and save humans and livestock. Most of the affected were nomadic communities of whom more than 200,000 had crossed the border into Uganda in search of pasture and water.[ii] In February 2017, the Current Food Insecurity Situation report presented to the Ugandan parliament indicated that 31% of the national population, or 10.9 million people, were food-insecure.[iii] In February 2017 the UN declared a famine in parts of South Sudan affecting 5 million people, in Somalia affecting one million and in Northern Nigeria.

The regularity with which these challenges happen is as alarming as the challenges themselves. In July 2011, the United Nations declared a famine in two regions of southern Somalia owing to what then was the worst drought in decades.[iv]

The lack of arable lands (which make up 22% of Africa's land surface) continues to be a problem, as more of this land is used for urban development, road and telecommunication networks, and the cultivation of non-food crops. Declaring that "Africa is its [own] worst environmental enemy," *The East African* newspaper argued that "many African leaders have failed to find any meaningful solution to the problem of harmonizing all these disparate land uses for sustainable development."[v]

When 'natural' disasters come to Africa, they either find fertile ground to devastate communities, or there are hardly any mitigation measures. Landslides happen because poor people have no resort other than to cultivate in places that expose them to grave danger when they abuse the environmental order. Poverty means that their methods of cultivation and herding of animals are not environmentally-friendly. When floods come, there are no flood defences. Poor environmental management and unregulated urbanisation undermine ecologies, resulting in disasters like flooding, landslides, deforestation and desertification.

Fact:

Deforestation & Wetlands:

At the end of 1990, Africa had an estimated 528 million hectares, or 30% of the world's tropical forests. In several Sub-Saharan African countries, the rate of deforestation exceeded the global annual average of 0.8%. While deforestation in other parts of the world is mainly caused by commercial logging or cattle ranching, the leading causes in Africa are associated with human activity. Developing countries rely heavily on wood fuel, the major energy source for cooking and heating. In Africa, the statistics are striking: an estimated 90% of the entire continent's population uses fuel-wood for cooking, and in Sub-Saharan Africa, firewood and brush supply approximately 52% of all energy sources. Sitting alongside deforestation is the encroachment on and draining of swamps and wetlands, which unbalances the ecology as designed by the Creator. Wetlands regulate water flow, recharge ground water, store and release water, filter nutrients and other pollutants, stabilise shorelines and the microclimate and are of exceptional importance as habitats supporting biodiversity. One estimate puts the total area covered by papyrus swamps in Africa at 4,000km^2, but their extent is decreasing due to human encroachment and intensified land use changes around them. The swamps supply large amounts of organic nutrients to fringing waters, thus allowing an increase in animal and plant production at the swamp edge. Some of the biggest culprits are the churches, many of which tend to construct in wetlands in either ignorance or defiance of their God-given mandate of stewardship over created things.

Desertification:

- **Dry lands cover 65% of the continent.** One-third of this area is hyper-arid deserts and completely uninhabited, except in oases. The remaining two-thirds of the dry lands, which comprise arid and semi-arid lands, are home to about 400 million Africans.

- Africa also suffers from inherently low soil fertility as the bedrock consists of granites and gneiss. Most of the soils in Africa are characterised by a low proportion of clay, making them easy to work and also easy to lose.

- Every year, **Africa loses about 280 million tonnes of cereal crops** from about 105 million hectares of croplands. This can be prevented if soil erosion is curbed.

- Poverty-related agricultural practices are a major contributor to desertification. Continuous cultivation without adding supplements, overgrazing, lack of soil and water conservation structures, and indiscriminate bushfires aggravate the process of desertification.

- Africa is geologically very old. **Nearly one-third of the central plateau of Africa is over 600 million years old** (Pre-Cambrian age). The rest of the surface has sand and alluvial deposits of Pleistocene age (less than 2 million years old). Human activities in obtaining food, fibre, fuel and shelter have significantly altered the soil.

- Archaeological records claim that **arid areas of Africa have been getting drier for almost 5,000 years**. However, desertification is a coincidence of drought with the increasing pressures on fragile arid and semi-arid lands by greater numbers of people and livestock. This is accelerating land degradation.

- According to estimates, **319 million hectares of Africa are vulnerable to desertification** due to sand movement. Assessments done by FAO and UNEP suggest that the desert is moving at an annual rate of 5km in the semi-arid areas of West Africa.

- Desertification is happening at an estimated 20,000 hectares per annum. At least 70% of Ethiopia is prone to desertification, while in Kenya, around 80% of the land is threatened by desertification.

- The **Great Green Wall** is a pan-African proposal to plant a wall of trees at the southern edge of the Sahara Desert to battle desertification. The strip of land from Dakar to Djibouti is 15 km (9 miles) wide and 7,100 km (4,400 miles) long. It is an initiative from the African Union.

Conservation:

A lot of the biblical evidence in the book of Genesis points to the Garden of Eden being in Africa. Whatever the arguments, it remains a fact that when He created animals of the wild (Genesis 1:24-25), God placed many of the exotic creatures in Africa. Today, many of these creatures (of which the Lord "saw that it was good" – verse 25b) are threatened with extinction. The decrease in numbers and the consequent risk of extinction is the result of poaching, loss of habitat, displacement, and deforestation.

Endangered African animals[vi]:

- Elephants: A recent aerial survey revealed that the continental population had dropped by nearly a third between 2007 and 2014, to around 415,000 elephants (less than the members of your tribe!) because of poaching and loss of habitat. '*Current Biology*' reported in February 2017 that Gabon had lost 80% of it elephant population to poachers in just one decade

- African Penguin: Less than 72,000 left (less than the members of your clan!) because they get caught up in the nets of commercial fisheries, and in oil spills. Also known as black-footed penguin, it is the only penguin that breeds in Africa

- African Lion: There are 22,000 left in this 'king of beasts', mainly due to poisonings, hunting and loss of habitat. How will future generations envision the Lion of Judah, or that glorious moment when the lion will lie down with the lamb?

- Cheetahs: The fastest animal on earth has only 14,000 (the congregation of just one mega church) individuals left as a result of loss of habitat and human interference

- Black Rhinoceros: Hunted to near extinction for their horn, there are only 3,500 (a medium-sized church) black rhinos left

- African Wild Dog: Only 4,000 left, they are hunted for meat, and are succumbing to disease

- Pygmy Hippopotamus: About 1,500 (the 10 o'clock service congregation) left in the wild because of deforestation and hunting

- Mountain Gorilla: A census in 2011 showed that there are fewer than 900 (the size of your church's Sunday School) left in a tiny mountainous region in the corners where Uganda, Rwanda, and DR Congo meet. Threatened by deforestation, 'development', and human disease like flu, pneumonia and Ebola

- Ethiopian Wolf: Habitat loss and disease have left only 400 (like the Marrieds Fellowship) animals left

- White Antelope (Addax): Just 200 left (like a single Economics class at university) due to hunting and drought.

Prophetic Implication:

The poor management of the environment could lead to the extinction of animal and plant species. It is us, God's people, who are messing up His creation. God took His time – five days, from the Second Day to the Sixth Day – creating the physical earth and everything in it, but we are spoiling them. God created the water (Genesis 1:6; 1:10), the vegetation (1:11-12), fish and birds (1:20-21), livestock and wild animals (1:24-25), and for each and all of them, He pronounced Himself, scripture records: "AND GOD SAW THAT IT WAS GOOD".

God's Principle:

Man was created AFTER all the other things, and then God charged him with stewardship: "So God created man in His own image, in the image of God He created him; male and female He created them. God blessed them and said to them, "Be fruitful and increase in number; fill the earth and subdue it. Rule over the fish of the sea and the birds of the air and over every living creature that moves on the ground. " Then God said, "I give you every seed-bearing plant on the face of the whole earth and every tree that has fruit with seed in it. They will be yours for food. And to all the beasts of the earth and all the birds of the air and all the creatures that move on the ground— everything that has the breath of life in it—I give every green plant for food." And it was so. God saw all that he had made, and it was very good. And there was evening, and there was morning — the sixth day." (Genesis 1:27-31)

Stewardship is the cardinal responsibility God gave to man for His creation of nature. In contemporary terms this is known as environmental conservation and ecological management. It is the first directive God gave to man.

Prayer Points:

1. Repentance

2. _____

3. _____

4. _____

5. _____

6. _____

7. _____

(Endnotes)

i   The Guardian, London

ii   The Star, Nairobi

iii The New Vision, Kampala

iv UN News Centre

v   World Press Review (VOL. 49, No. 10)

vi Emeka Chigozie, AnswersAfrica

CHAPTER NINE

Plague of Locusts (Graft & Corruption)

Pharaonic Confrontation:

Exodus 10:1-20 Now the Lord said to Moses, "Go in to Pharaoh; for I have hardened his heart and the hearts of his servants, that I may show these signs of Mine before him, ² and that you may tell in the hearing of your son and your son's son the mighty things I have done in Egypt, and My signs which I have done among them, that you may know that I *am* the Lord."

³ So Moses and Aaron came in to Pharaoh and said to him, "Thus says the LORD God of the Hebrews: 'How long will you refuse to humble yourself before Me? Let My people go, that they may serve Me. ⁴ Or else, if you refuse to let My people go, behold, tomorrow I will bring locusts into your territory. ⁵ And they shall cover the face of the earth, so that no one will be able to see the earth; and they shall eat the residue of what is left, which remains to you from the hail, and they shall eat every tree which grows up for you out of the field. ⁶ They shall fill your houses, the houses of all your servants, and the houses of

all the Egyptians—which neither your fathers nor your fathers' fathers have seen, since the day that they were on the earth to this day.'" And he turned and went out from Pharaoh.

7 Then Pharaoh's servants said to him, "How long shall this man be a snare to us? Let the men go, that they may serve the LORD their God. Do you not yet know that Egypt is destroyed?" 8 So Moses and Aaron were brought again to Pharaoh, and he said to them, "Go, serve the LORD YOUR GOD. WHO *are* the ones that are going?"

9 And Moses said, "We will go with our young and our old; with our sons and our daughters, with our flocks and our herds we will go, for we must hold a feast to the LORD." 10 Then he said to them, "The LORD had better be with you when I let you and your little ones go! Beware, for evil is ahead of you. 11 Not so! Go now, you *who are* men, and serve the LORD, for that is what you desired." And they were driven out from Pharaoh's presence.

12 Then the LORD said to Moses, "Stretch out your hand over the land of Egypt for the locusts, that they may come upon the land of Egypt, and eat every herb of the land—all that the hail has left." 13 So Moses stretched out his rod over the land of Egypt, and the LORD brought an east wind on the land all that day and all *that* night. When it was morning, the east wind brought the locusts. 14 And the locusts went up over all the land of Egypt and rested on all the territory of Egypt. *They were* very severe; previously there had been no such locusts as they, nor shall there be such after them. 15 For they covered the face of the whole earth, so that the land was darkened; and they ate every herb of the land and all the fruit of the trees which the hail had left. So there remained nothing

green on the trees or on the plants of the field throughout all the land of Egypt.

[16] Then Pharaoh called for Moses and Aaron in haste, and said, "I have sinned against the LORD your God and against you. [17] Now therefore, please forgive my sin only this once, and entreat the LORD your God, that He may take away from me this death only." [18] So he went out from Pharaoh and entreated the LORD. [19] And the LORD turned a very strong west wind, which took the locusts away and blew them into the Red Sea. There remained not one locust in all the territory of Egypt. [20] But the LORD hardened Pharaoh's heart, and he did not let the children of Israel go.

Post-Exodus Judgment:

Isaiah 19:14 "The LORD has poured into them a spirit of dizziness; they make Egypt stagger in all that she does, as a drunkard staggers around in his vomit."

Snapshot: (Children and Adults Alike)

Corruption has made a mockery of polling exercises across the continent. Not only are national and general elections characterised by vote-rigging and inducements of voters, but even polling in schools for class prefects and student leadership is increasingly being typified by voter inducement of items life sweets and candy. Exam-cheating is rife in schools, as is the sex-for-marks relationship between students and lecturers at university. The election and instalment of church leaders has also been penetrated by corrupt interests. Manifestation in schools and church signifies the depth to which corruption has eaten away at the fabric of society, like locusts consuming everything in sight. This is on top of the graft-induced awarding of business tenders, tax avoidance, or substandard performance of public works and services, and the theft of public funds which is euphemistically called embezzlement. Corruption is also evident in the supposedly smaller matters like the flouting of basic rules such as traffic regulations, time-keeping, tithing, and jumping of queues.

Transparency International's African edition of the Global Corruption Barometer for 2015 spoke to 43,143 respondents across 28 countries in Sub-Saharan Africa. They were asked about their experiences and perceptions of corruption in their country. Nearly 75 million people had paid a bribe in the past year – some of these to escape punishment by the police or courts, but many also forced to pay to get access to the basic services that they desperately need. A majority of Africans perceive corruption to be on the rise and think that their government is failing in its efforts to fight corruption; and many also feel disempowered as regards to taking action against corruption. Sierra Leoneans, Nigerians, Liberians and Ghanaians are the most negative about the scale of corruption in their country.[i]

Around 80% of African people live on less than $2 a day. Corruption is one factor perpetuating poverty. Poverty and corruption combine to force people to make impossible choices like "Do I buy food for my family today or do I pay a bribe to get treated at the clinic?" Poor people often have low access to education and can remain uninformed about their rights, leaving them more easily exploited and excluded.[ii]

In a Transparency International survey in 28 countries in sub-Saharan Africa in 2014, 22% of Africans who had contact with public services admitted to having paid a bribe in the past year. In Liberia the figure was 69%. In Kenya and Nigeria it was 37% and 43% respectively. Across the continent, a majority of respondents said that they thought corruption had got worse in their country in the past year. In South Africa, the figure was 83%.

Fact:

On the eve of stepping down from the presidency of South Africa in 1999, President Nelson Mandela lamented: "We came to government with the zeal of a group of people who were going to eliminate corruption in government. It was such a disappointment to note that our own people who are there to wipe out corruption themselves became corrupt."[iii]

In Transparency International's 2016 Corruption Index, which ranked 176 countries from least corrupt to most corrupt, 12 of the 20 ranked worst were African. Somalia (176), South Sudan (175), Sudan (170), Libya (170), Guinea-Bissau (168), Eritrea (164), Angola (164), Republic of Congo (159), Chad(159), Central African Republic(159), Burundi (159), Democratic Republic of Congo (156) featured at the wrong end of the index with the best-ranked Africans being in the not-so-creditable positions of Botswana (35), Cape Verde (38), Mauritius (50) and Rwanda (50).

Prophetic Implication:

Like locusts, corruption eats up everything in its way, leaving nothing untouched. Corruption and 'eating' go on with such vigour that the eaters do not realise that they have become dizzy with greed. Yet at the end of it all, they will vomit the proceeds of their gluttony.

Exodus 10:15 "They covered ALL THE GROUND until it was BLACK. They devoured all that was left after the hail—everything growing in the fields and the FRUIT on the trees. Nothing GREEN remained on TREE or plant in all the land of Egypt."

Prophetic Symbols

'Ground' is territory, entire institutions, systems, or nations. The experience of places that have been hit by corruption is that it is all-enveloping.

'Black' is scarcity or famine[iv]. Much of the famine in Africa has been caused by graft.

'Fruit' is a source of nourishment, reward for labour, harvest and it is fullness. All these have been eaten by graft.

'Green' is life and provision. The richness of life is represented in its viridescence.

'Tree' stands for a leader, or person or organisation. It could be a kingdom or a nation. Corruption has infested our leaders, organisations, systems, and nations. Trees have been stripped bare.

'Vomit' stands for the "unpleasant return of ill-gotten things".[v]

<u>God's Principle:</u>

The wealth of the sinner is laid up for the just: the corrupt will vomit their ill-gotten wealth, which the Lord will allocate to the righteous (Proverbs 13:22b). For the uncompromisingly righteous, God has immense wealth reserved for his use prior to the second coming of

Jesus. "To the man who pleases Him, God gives wisdom, knowledge and happiness, but to the sinner He gives the task of gathering and storing up wealth to hand it over to the one who pleases God" (Ecclesiastes 2:26).

When a nation exalts God, God will exalt that nation. It is God Who "removes kings and sets up kings," (Dan 2:21) and the nations are nothing to Him.

Proverbs 29:2 "When the righteous increase, the people rejoice, but when the wicked rule, the people groan." We don't have to look very far to find historical accounts where corruption brought down a nation. Just prior to the fall of Rome, there was so much corruption that few even cared to hide it. It was even joked about. Is there any doubt that political, governmental, and corporate corruption are at an all-time high?

Ephesians 5:11 "Take no part in the unfruitful works of darkness, but instead expose them." The Bible is absolutely clear about how Christians must react to such things when exposed to them (at work, private, wherever). We are to have "no part" or take no part in it, meaning not even a little, and tiny part. Having *"no part"* means avoiding the *"works of darkness"* altogether, and that means avoiding those who do them. In fact, we're told to expose them, because whoever breaks man's laws, also breaks God's laws (Rom 13:1-5), and if you break God's laws, in time, they'll break you (and me) too.

Isaiah 1:4 "Ah, sinful nation, a people laden with iniquity, offspring of evildoers, children who deal corruptly!" The same applies to any nation whose people are laden with sin. God is no respecter of persons or nations and what He did to Israel in His righteous judgment He can do to any nation. The consequences for Israel would be the same for any nation that is laden with iniquity; it will lead to God's judgment; unless they repent.

Prayer Points:

1. Repentance

2. _____

3. _____

4. _____

5. _____

6. _____

7. _____

(Endnotes)

i   Transparency International, Global Corruption Barometer, 2015

ii   Transparency International

iii Martin Meredith, *'The Fortunes of Africa'*. Simon & Schuster, London, 2014

iv   Joe Ibojie, *Bible-based Dictionary of Prophetic Symbols for Every Christian*. Cross House Books, Aberdeen, 2009

v   Ibid.

CHAPTER TEN

Plague of Darkness (Ignorance)

Pharaonic Confrontation:

Exodus 10:21-29 Then the LORD said to Moses, "Stretch out your hand toward the sky so that darkness will spread over Egypt—darkness that can be felt." So Moses stretched out his hand toward the sky, and total darkness covered all Egypt for three days. No one could see anyone else or leave his place for three days. Yet all the Israelites had light in the places where they lived. Then Pharaoh summoned Moses and said, "Go, worship the LORD. Even your women and children may go with you; only leave your flocks and herds behind." But Moses said, "You must allow us to have sacrifices and burnt offerings to present to the LORD our God. Our livestock too must go with us; not a hoof is to be left behind. We have to use some of them in worshiping the LORD our God, and until we get there we will not know what we are to use to worship the LORD." But the LORD hardened Pharaoh's heart, and he was not willing to let them go. Pharaoh said to Moses, "Get out of my sight! Make sure you do not appear before me again! The day you see my face you will die." "Just as you say," Moses replied, "I will never appear before you again."

Post-Exodus Judgment:

Isaiah 19:11-13 "The officials of Zoan are nothing but fools; the wise counselors of Pharaoh give senseless advice. How can you say to Pharaoh, "I am one of the wise men, a disciple of the ancient kings"? Where are your wise men now? Let them show you and make known what the LORD Almighty has planned against Egypt. The officials of Zoan have become fools, the leaders of Memphis are deceived; the cornerstones of her peoples have led Egypt astray."

Snapshot: (Few Inventions, Little Innovation, Foreign Philosophies)

Africa hardly invents nor innovates, and yet the progress of mankind depends a lot on technological and sociological innovation. Nearly all technologies that Africa uses have been invented and innovated elsewhere. Nearly all systems – democracy & electoral politics, accounting systems, army rankings, government & administrative structures, banking regulations – that Africa uses have been innovated elsewhere and appropriated wholesale on the continent.

Africa is easily the least inventive of the world's continents, contributing little to scientific scholarship, or to historical, geographical or anthropological knowledge. Very few patents are filed out of Africa. For science, money is just one of many problems; labs are poorly equipped, and science students get little practical research training because research centres are often separate from universities.

UNESCO noted in 2010 that while this continent is "replete with natural resources, intellectual capital, indigenous knowledge and culture, Africa is nevertheless at a comparative disadvantage when it comes to overall development because of its low investment in science and technology (S&T). This results in poor infrastructure development, a small pool of researchers and minimal scientific output. The continent has often adopted a short-term view of human development, persisting in a reliance on external financial support, which often targets short-term goals. As a result, the continent has failed to invest in science, technology and innovation (STI) as drivers of economic growth and long-term sustainable development."[i]

Africa tends to be an uncritical consumer of foreign-imposed philosophies that find their way, unfiltered, into national education curricular, health programmes, administrative and management systems, and in development aid projects. Many of the philosophies subscribe to New Age and Eastern religion. Many leaders and managers, focussed on self-preservation and personal aggrandisement, become unwitting conduits for dangerous philosophies that undermine the spiritual integrity of our nations.

Fact:

Africa's ratio of scientists per million people is less than 85:1,000,000,[ii] compared to 4,500 per million people in the United States and 656 in Brazil.

Africa produces a very tiny percentage of global scientific knowledge. [iii] Sub-Saharan Africa produced just 11,142 scientific articles in 2008, which was 1.1% of world output. Within the continent, South Africa produced almost half (46.4%) of the total, followed by Nigeria (11.4%) and Kenya (6.6%).[iv] In other words, these three countries alone produce two-thirds of the continent's scientific articles.

Most African countries were unable to produce 100 publications in the natural sciences in 2008. These figures are well below the theoretical threshold that would trigger a virtuous interaction between science and technology (S&T). This threshold was in the neighbourhood of 150 papers per million population in 1998 and has since risen.[v]

In 2006, members of the African Union endorsed a target for each nation to spend 1% of its gross domestic product (GDP) on research and development (R&D). In May 2011, the African Union released African Innovation Outlook 2010, a survey of some of the scientifically most productive sub-Saharan nations. It showed that only three — Malawi, Uganda and South Africa — topped the 1% spending threshold in 2007; most remained far from that mark, even when the support from foreign donors was included.[vi]

The African University of Science and Technology [vii] (AUST) was founded to address gaps on the continent. Conceived by Africans across the continent and from the diaspora, with major support from the World Bank Institute (WBI), AUST was established as a regional initiative by the Nelson Mandela Institution (NMI, Inc.) in 2007. Its goal was and remains the creation of world class research and advanced training institutes in relevant scientific and technological disciplines which would serve as regional resources and centres of excellence in sub-Saharan Africa.

Prophetic Implication:

The wisdom of the '-isms' (Capitalism, Socialism, Communism, Fascism, Nationalism, Feudalism, Pan-Africanism) is foolishness.

The word *knowledge* in the Bible denotes an understanding, a recognition, or an acknowledgment. To "know" something is to perceive it or to be aware of it. Many times in Scripture, knowledge carries the idea of a deeper appreciation of something or a relationship with someone.

Zoan and Memphis were the current (in Isaiah's time) and the ancient capitals of Egypt. Capital cities, by definition, harbour all the wise people who proclaim and administer the policies that run nations. The Word of the Lord is saying that the leaders and the officials are foolish and have deceptive knowledge.

The Seven Spirits of God (Isaiah 11:2-3) are presented in three pairs plus one. The spirit of knowledge is introduced with the spirit of the fear of the Lord. The pairings are each essential for particular roles or ministry:

- *Wisdom* and *Understanding* for government

- *Counsel* and *Power* for war

- *Knowledge* and *Fear of the Lord* for spiritual leadership

- (*Delight in the Fear of the Lord* for worship)

The history of mankind teaches us that the nations that have had more knowledge relative to others have, naturally, been leaders of the world. For Africa to assume its prophetic leadership role to be "a blessing on the earth" (Isaiah 19:23-25), there will have to be a big up-kick of its knowledge base.

God's Principle:

The Lord is concerned about the deadly effects of ignorance or the absence of knowledge, and then He Himself pledges that there will be consequences thereof for the work of the current age and for future generations: "My people are destroyed from lack of knowledge. 'Because you have rejected knowledge, I also reject you as my priests; because you have ignored the law of your God, I also will ignore your children.'" (Hosea 4:6)

Human knowledge, apart from God, is flawed. Chasing after knowledge for its own sake, without seeking God, is foolishness. That is why the "fear of the Lord" is critical.

Knowledge is a gift from God. "For the LORD gives wisdom, and from his mouth come knowledge and understanding" (Proverbs 2:6). God gives the gift of knowledge out of His infinite store of knowledge. He knows everything: what was, what is, what could be, what might have been, what will be – and all the hows, whys, whos and whens associated therewith.

Scientific knowledge, or the study of nature, is central to God's infinite store: the heavens and the skies, so well-spoken of in Psalm 19, are repositories of a lot of scientific knowledge, including space, time, weather, and astronomy. "The heavens declare the glory of God; the skies proclaim the work of his hands. Day after day they pour forth speech; night after night they display knowledge" (Psalm 19:1-2). It is a good place for Africans to go to. They would first have to fear the Lord.

Plague of Darkness (Ignorance)

Prayer Points:

1.   Repentance

2.   _____

3.   _____

4.   _____

5.   _____

6.   _____

7.   _____

(Endnotes)

i   UNESCO Science Report, 2010. *'The Current Status of Science around the World'*

ii   African University of Science and Technology, Abuja, Nigeria

iii   World Economic Forum

iv   Ibid.

v   Ibid.

vi   Nature: International Weekly Journal of Science, June 2011

vii   African University of Science and Technology, Abuja, Nigeria

CHAPTER ELEVEN

Plague *on* the Firstborn
(Generations & Mineral Wealth)

Pharaonic Confrontation:

Exodus 11:1-10   Now the LORD had said to Moses, "I will bring one more plague on Pharaoh and on Egypt. After that, he will let you go from here, and when he does, he will drive you out completely. Tell the people that men and women alike are to ask their neighbours for articles of silver and gold." (The LORD made the Egyptians favourably disposed toward the people, and Moses himself was highly regarded in Egypt by Pharaoh's officials and by the people.) So Moses said, "This is what the LORD says: 'About midnight I will go throughout Egypt. Every firstborn son in Egypt will die, from the firstborn son of Pharaoh, who sits on the throne, to the firstborn son of the female slave, who is at her hand mill, and all the firstborn of the cattle as well. There will be loud wailing throughout Egypt—worse than there has ever been or ever will be again. But among the Israelites not a dog will bark at any person or animal.' Then you will know that the LORD makes a distinction between Egypt and Israel.

All these officials of yours will come to me, bowing down before me and saying, 'Go, you and all the people who follow you!' After that I will leave." Then Moses, hot with anger, left Pharaoh. The LORD had said to Moses, "Pharaoh will refuse to listen to you—so that my wonders may be multiplied in Egypt."

Moses and Aaron performed all these wonders before Pharaoh, but the LORD hardened Pharaoh's heart, and he would not let the Israelites go out of his country.

Post-Exodus Judgment:

Isaiah 19:15-17 "There is nothing Egypt can do – head or tail, palm branch or reed. In that day the Egyptians will be like women. They will shudder with fear at the uplifted hand that the LORD Almighty raises against them. And the land of Judah will bring terror to the Egyptians; everyone to whom Judah is mentioned will be terrified, because of what the LORD Almighty is planning against them."

Snapshot: (Despising her Inheritance)

The Plague on the Firstborn was pronounced on both people (families/generations) and on cattle (economic well-being). In complement, there was also the 'voluntary' loss of precious items of silver and gold (Exodus 11:2), which symbolise the kind of prosperity that mineral wealth brings to nations. This final judgment is particularly poignant for Africa, home to the Garden of Eden because, like Esau the firstborn son of Isaac, Africa has despised her inheritance by thoughtlessly giving away the natural resources that would have been building blocks for her economies. Africa, much more than other continents and regions, has allowed others to ship away its minerals and hydrocarbons, and not used them to transform her economies.

Fact:

Most of Africa's natural resources are simply exported raw, with little attempt by the generations that have been up to now to convert these resources into productive capital. Instead of sowing the seed, the seed is simply eaten through raw commodity export to raise revenues for immediate consumption. It is what Esau did. And it is the main factor behind Africa's poverty and economic stagnation, relative to other regions.

Following is the situation with Africa's mineral and hydrocarbon resources[i]:

- Africa has about 30% of the world's known reserves of minerals (with just 10% of its population and only 1% of international trade)

- Africa has about 10% of the world's oil and 8% of gas resources

- Africa has the largest cobalt, diamonds, platinum, and uranium reserves in the world

- Africa's minerals have a comparably low level of exploration

- In 2012, mining, oil and gas accounted for 28% of the continent's GDP

- In 2012, natural resources accounted for 77% of total exports and 42% of government revenues.

Prophetic Implication:

The "firstborn son in Egypt" (Exodus 11:5a) is represent-ative of the first generations of Africa. These have essentially lost out and not been beneficiaries of the promise in the prophecy contained in Isaiah 19:22 that says that "they will turn to the LORD, and He will respond to their pleas and heal them", which will come after the "altar to the Lord in the heart of Egypt" (verse 19) has been established. That firstborn son is the generations that have been up to date.

The "firstborn of the cattle" (Exodus 11:5b) is what God gave as the first economic provision for the nations. Water excepted, the first major provision that the Lord prepared for man's sustenance was "the dry ground 'land'" (Genesis 1:10). It is land that contains all the minerals and hydrocarbons that, in the last 200 years, have been pivotal for the economic advancement of the nations. Land and its first offspring of minerals was created (Genesis 1:10) before the other economic provisions like seed-bearing plants for agriculture (Genesis 1:11), fish (Genesis 1:20-21), domestic animals (Genesis 1:24), and let alone man himself (Genesis 1:26-27). Geologically speaking, the minerals and hydrocarbons that we mine and extract from the ground today are millions of years old, much older than the various living things around us, including ourselves.

As part of the judgment pronounced in the form of the final plague, Egypt was to give up their "articles of gold and silver" (Exodus 11:2). In the Scripture, the Lord's judgment on the surrender of these precious metals is preceded, in Exodus 11:2a by the directive that the Israelites were "to ask their Egyptian neighbours", and is then followed by the revelation, rendered in parentheses, that "(the Lord made the Egyptians favourably disposed towards the people [Israelites])" (Exodus 11:3), which presumes that the Egyptians handed over their valuables willingly. This is confirmed at the moment of departure, when the exodus gets underway: "The Israelites did as Moses instructed and asked the Egyptians for articles of silver and gold and for clothing. The LORD had made the Egyptians favorably disposed toward the people, and they gave them what they asked for; so they plundered the Egyptians." (Exodus 12:35-36)

This is exactly what has been happening to Africa in regard to its minerals and hydrocarbons inheritance. Africa has been surrendering them "willingly", and the others have used them for their own economic advancement. African countries wilfully concession away their mineral resources to others for a pittance, like Esau did. It so happens that the first major tectonic shift in the economic fortunes of organised society came with the Industrial Revolution, which was built on the foundations of the judicious use of mineral resources. Such was the impact of the Industrial Revolution that one scholar wrote that the changes over 200 years since the Industrial Revolution began exceeded those of the preceding 7,000 years.

A big transfer of resources from Africa/Egypt was promised to Abraham that it would happen after Israel had served 400 years in Egypt (Genesis 15:14; Psalms 105:37).

"There is nothing Egypt can do" (Isaiah 19:15a/NIV): There is no lucrative, society-transforming trade or business to carry on, says the scripture; there is simply economic stagnation across the entire continent. This is the place where Africa has been over thousands of years.

"Head or tail, palm branch or reed" (Isaiah 19:15b) is a figurative description of the classes of the people and the structure of the nation. The 'head' stands for the government or national authority. These can do nothing, and neither can the 'tail', which represents the general population. The 'branch' as a prophetic symbol stands for the Church, or God's people[ii], and the 'reed' is the systems on which they stand. These too can do nothing except that they repent.

"Neither shall there be any work" (Isaiah 19:15a/NKJV) - the sense is that there shall be such discord that no man, whether a prince, a politician, or a priest, shall be able to give any advice, or form any plan for the national safety and security, which shall be successful.[iii]

"In that day the Egyptians will be like women" (Isaiah 19:16), feeble and fearful. The cowardice and effeminacy of the nation in general, joined with the people's fear and trepidation, are here set forth as a second cause of their calamity; and the reason of this, among other things, is drawn from a sense of the divine judgment. The nations of Africa have, because of their lowly economic status, been consistently weak in the face of other nations.

God's Principle:

The Lord is a God of redemption. To redeem the people and the nations is part of Jesus' mission statement: "The Spirit of the Lord is on me, because he has anointed me to proclaim good news to the poor. He has sent me to proclaim freedom for the prisoners and recovery of sight for the blind, to set the oppressed free, to proclaim the year of the Lord's favour" (Luke 4:18-19). Africa is poor, as we have seen with the Plague on Livestock; it is blind, as witnessed in the Plague of Darkness. The time of the Lord's favour is at hand, as prophesied in Isaiah 19:19-25.

The prerequisite step is repentance. Because as the God of the Covenant He is faithful to the word that He has pronounced through the prophets, God will fulfil it. It is up to the Church to pray these promises into being, or to prayerfully discern when the time has come for the fulfilment of a prophetic promise.

Prayer Points:

1. Repentance

2. _____

3. _____

4. _____

5. _____

6. _____

7. _____

(Endnotes)

i   African Natural Resources Center (ANRC), a non-lending entity of the African Development Bank (AfDB)

ii   Joe Ibojie, *Bible-based Dictionary of Prophetic Symbols for Every Christian.* Cross House Books, Aberdeen, 2009

iii Barnes' Notes on the Bible

CHAPTER TWELVE

How Will Africa Overcome?

The Proclamation against Egypt in Isaiah 19 shows that Africa was/is under judgment. Frequently we only appropriate the latter part of this passage, verses 19-25, the prophecy of Africa's redemptive role which Scripture says will be done in concert with Israel and Assyria (Arab world), and we exclude the earlier part of the prophecy, which actually is judgment.

We have seen how the plagues of the Exodus were reflected in the judgments pronounced through the Prophet Isaiah in Isaiah 19:1-18. The two events took place more than 700 years apart, for the Exodus happened in 1446 BC, while the ministry of Isaiah, the greatest of the writing prophets, went on up to 681 BC, when he died.

The implication of the seven-century spacing, then, is that:

1. The ten plagues were not a one-off event that was limited to the nine months of the year 1446 BC when the signs and wonders were enacted in Pharaoh's Egypt. That the frogs died; the flies left; the thunder

stopped; no locust was left; the firstborn died, are all but the physical manifestations that were necessary for Israel's redemption. The spiritual manifestation is what we need to be discerning of

2. When the Lord pronounced the oracle concerning Egypt many centuries later through His servant Isaiah, it meant that the consequences of the judgment were still alive centuries later

3. The challenge then, for Africa today, is to discern whether in the years that have passed since Isaiah's pronouncement up to today, 2017 AD, these judgments have lived on

4. Given that Isaiah 19:1-18 leads directly, both in sequence and in consequence, to Isaiah 19:19-25 that pronounces Africa's future prophetic role as a "blessing on the earth" (verse 24), which has not yet been fulfilled, it follows then that the effects of the judgment should still be alive.

If we agree that the judgments have lived on for almost 3,000 years, this then in summary is the place of Africa today as was prophetically pronounced in Isaiah 19:1-18:

Verse 2: Internal strife, war and chaos

Verse 3: Idolatry taking over in the land; with nowhere to turn, Africans are consulting spiritualists

Verse 4: Bad rule – from being dominated by foreign powers, as happened with colonialism, or by bad rulers like the kings of the past who sold nations for a ransom, on to post-Independence dictatorships, Africa has been having a much bigger share of poor and cruel leadership than other regions of the world

Verses 5-10: The economies are suffering in numerous ways – a parched environment, lack of productivity, dissatisfied workers, little or no return on investment

Verses 11-14: Leadership – policies and advice have come to nought. Government advisers, multilateral partners and donors' aid have all come to nothing. Legislators' wisdom is nothing

Verse 15: No one has any answer – not the head (the Presidents, Prime Ministers, Cabinets), nor the tail (ordinary citizens). Neither the palm branch (the Church)), nor the reed/bulrush (institutions of government and state; the pillars on which these institutions stand) can do much. The answers, ultimately, lie in the Lord, where Africa's undivided allegiance must go (verse 18), if we are to overcome.

But in order to plot the way forward, we need to go back to the respective beginnings of the plagues and the judgment in the two books of Exodus and Isaiah to understand what exactly we are up against.

Even before they start being referred to as "plagues", the Lord God, when briefing Moses, calls them "miraculous signs and wonders". In outlining the assignment, including Aaron's role, the Lord tells Moses: "See, I have made you like God to Pharaoh, and your brother Aaron will be your prophet. You are to say everything I command you, and your brother Aaron is to tell Pharaoh to let the Israelites go out of his country. But I will harden Pharaoh's heart, and though I multiply my **miraculous signs and wonders** in Egypt, he will not listen to you. Then I will lay my hand on Egypt and with mighty acts of judgment I will bring out my divisions, my people the Israelites." (Exodus 7:1-4).

Spiritual Warfare

The first sign and wonder is when Aaron's staff becomes a snake. But Pharaoh calls in his sorcerers whose secret arts include tossing up snakes. Aaron's staff swallows their staffs, praise the Lord, but the significance of it all is that the devil was present, for the snakes of the secret arts denote Satan. Since the devil was there at this starting point, we know that the way to overcome him is by spiritual warfare.

Repentance

The judgments of Isaiah 19:1-18 are introduced thus: "See, the LORD rides on a swift cloud and is coming to Egypt." Clouds are vehicles for the Lord's coming to execute judgment (Psalm 18:10-11; Psalm 104:3; Daniel 7:13). Since the Lord's throne is established on righteous and justice (Psalm 89:14), it follows that if He is coming to execute judgement on Egypt/Africa then we, Africans, are guilty. No other way is given for the forgiveness of our guilt than that we should repent.

In Exodus 12:12 God speaks of executing judgment on all the gods of Egypt. He says: "On that same night I will pass through Egypt and strike down every firstborn - both men and animals - and I will bring judgment on all the gods of Egypt. I am the LORD."

In some measure He had already done so in the plagues, as Egypt's gods were very much tied up with the forces of nature. Ha'pi, the Nile-god of inundation, had brought not prosperity but ruin; the frogs, symbol of Heqit, a goddess of fruitfulness, had brought only disease and wasting; the hail, rain and storm were supposed to be heralds of awesome events, and the sun-god Re had been bloated out.[i] Their dedications were abominable before God, for Pharaoh's Egypt "worshipped and served created things rather than the Creator" (Romans 1:25). The same thing is still happening across Africa today, where created things are deified.

One great and appropriate cry of penitence is:

> "Now therefore, O our God, the great, mighty and awesome God, who keeps his covenant of love, do not let all this hardship seem trifling in Your eyes--the hardship that has come upon us, upon our kings and leaders, upon our priests and prophets, upon our fathers and all Your people, from the days of the kings of Assyria until today. In all that has happened to us, You have been just; You have acted faithfully, while we did wrong. Our kings, our leaders, our priests and our fathers did not follow Your law; they did not pay attention to Your commands or the warnings You gave them. Even while they were in their kingdom, enjoying Your great goodness to them in the spacious and fertile land You gave them, they did not serve You or turn from their evil ways. "But see, we are slaves today, slaves in the land You gave our forefathers so they could eat its fruit and the other good things it produces. Because of our sins, its abundant harvest goes to the kings You have placed over us. They rule over our bodies and our cattle as they please. We are in great distress." (Nehemiah 9:32-37)

Petition & Intercession

The first nine plagues in the book of Exodus can be divided into three groups of 3. That would be 7:14 to 8:19; 8:20 to9:12; 9:13 to 10:29, with the first plague in each group (that is the first, the fourth and the seventh) introduced by a warning delivered to Pharaoh in the morning as he went out to the Nile.[ii] Pharaoh was very hardened of heart, either of his own pig-headedness or because the Lord stiffened him. The pharaohs of today, the leaders of Africa, can be unyielding too to the things of the Living God. Prayer and petition must be made, for "intercession and thanksgiving be made for everyone - for kings and all those in authority, that we may live peaceful and quiet lives" (1 Timothy 2:1-2). A cry must go out to the Lord to "remove from you your heart of stone and give you a heart of flesh" (Ezekiel 36:26.

A Charge to the Prophets of Africa: Prophets will have a critical role to play in Africa's redemption (Exodus 7:1). The staff that Moses and Aaron used is representative of authority. Jesus, the Chief Shepherd, uses a staff to guide His flock. Aaron's staff swallowed the staffs of the magicians and sorcerers, so victory is assured for us.

When Israel was released from captivity and set apart from the debilitating effects of the plagues, the Israelites broke forth and went on to become the most important nation on earth – not just the state of Israel, but the nation of the Jews becoming the most influential people on earth. The promise to Israel conveyed through the Prophet Micah can be appropriated by Africa as well: "The day for building your walls will come, the day for extending your boundaries. In that day people will come to you from Assyria and the cities of Egypt, even from

Egypt to the Euphrates and from sea to sea and from mountain to mountain. The earth will become desolate because of its inhabitants, as the result of their deeds. Shepherd your people with your staff, the flock of your inheritance, which lives by itself in a forest, in fertile pasturelands" (Micah 7:11-14).

Africa is still being held back by the ten plagues. It will need to break free from the plagues in order to meet its prophetic destiny as revealed in Isaiah 19:19-25. After that it will then take the redemption of the Assyrians (Arabs) before the fulfilment of the blessing that Egypt (God's people – Isaiah 19:20), Assyria (God's handiwork - Isaiah 19:20), and Israel (God's inheritance - Isaiah 19:20), the tripartite blessings, come to the earth. Africans should not seek solutions overseas, where many have either escaped to, looking for visas and green cards, or seeking the wisdom of others, in so defying the Lord's will: "He made every nation of men, that they should inhabit the whole earth; and He determined the times set for them and the exact places where they should live. God did this so that men would seek Him and perhaps reach out for Him and find Him, though He is not far from each one of us" (Acts 17:26-27).

ENDS

(Endnotes)

i   New Bible Dictionary. Inter-Varsity Press, Leicester, England/ Downers Grove. Illinois, USA

ii   Study Notes, The NIV Study Bible. The Zondervan Corporation, 1985

Other books by David Sseppuuya

1. **Africa's Industrialisation & Prosperity** – From Esau Syndrome to Structural Adjustment Strategy

2. **Uganda, Africa & Israel:** Prophetic Implications of Historical, Geographical and Divine Links

www.ingramcontent.com/pod-product-compliance
Lightning Source LLC
Chambersburg PA
CBHW052128090426
42741CB00009B/2004